Joan K. Parry, DSW
Editor

From Prevention to Wellness Through Group Work

Pre-publication
REVIEWS,
COMMENTARIES,
EVALUATIONS . . .

"**T**his volume offers a rich collection of ideas on social group work practice, providing a well-grounded integration of philosophy and theory with creative group programs and activities. Each chapter captures one's imagination by offering a different, yet related, facet of social group work intervention. The practical nature of the discussions and the illustrations of practice processes provide a stimulating and encouraging boost to one's own efforts.

It is rewarding to see the integration of theory and basic practice philosophy with worker activity and successful individual and group outcomes. The selections demonstrate that a high level of social group work practice not only exists, but can be described in terms that make it accessible to beginning practitioners. Workers with the most needful group participants will uncover the marvelous capacity of the human spirit to grow and thrive through the social processes of small group participation.

Some nice additions to the collection are Alice Home's discussion of the integration of practice and research and Cyrus S Behroozi's analysis of structural impediments to the inclusion of social group work practice content in the social work curriculum.

This collection well illustrates the theme of the symposium on which it is based, 'From Prevention to Wellness Through Group Work.'

Elizabeth Lewis, PhD
Professor Emerita,
Department of Social Work,
Cleveland State University

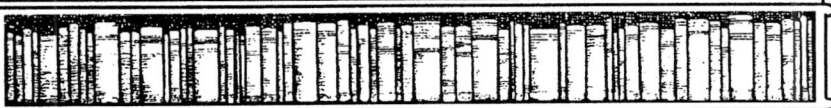

More pre-publication
REVIEWS, COMMENTARIES, EVALUATIONS . . .

"**F**rom Prevention to Wellness Through Group Work includes a wide range of articles addressing approaches, issues, and populations in group work practice. Constructivism, empowerment, psycho-education, conflict, scapegoating, the homeless, the elderly, persons with AIDS, and children with emotional disabilities are some of the book's subjects.

The article by Gale Goldberg-Wood and Ruth R. Middleman on constructivism and group work is especially thought-provoking and original. The contribution by Marcia B. Cohen and Julie M. Johnson about a community poetry group for homeless people is quite beautiful and the work of George S. Getzel on services with people with AIDS is an excellent discussion of social group work with this population.

The book well reflects group work practice with vulnerable populations. Both practitioners and educators will find interesting material here."

Roselle Kurland, PhD
Professor, Hunter College
School of Social Work;
Editor, Social Work with Groups

"**C**learly and incisively written, the chapters in this book include the very best presentations from the 17th annual AASWG symposium. The book expands and enriches social work practice with groups by focusing on prevention, wellness, and the empowerment of people and societies as the field of social work approaches the twenty-first century. Including far-ranging content on group work practice with children, youth, adults, and older adults, *From Prevention to Wellness Through Group Work* is essential reading for anyone interested in the empowerment of vulnerable populations by using prevention and wellness promotion strategies."

Ronald W. Toseland, PhD
Director and Professor,
Ringel Institute of Gerontology,
School of Social Welfare,
State University of New York
at Albany

The Haworth Press, Inc.

From Prevention to Wellness Through Group Work

HAWORTH Titles of Related Interest

Voices from the Field: Group Work Responds, Selected Proceedings of the 16th Annual Symposium of AASWG, edited by Albert S. Alissi and Catherine G. Corto Mergins

Group Work Practice in a Troubled Society: Problems and Opportunities, Selected Proceedings of the 15th Annual Symposium of AASWG, edited by Roselle Kurland and Robert Salmon

Social Group Work Today and Tomorrow: Moving from Theory to Advanced Training and Practice, Selected Proceedings of the 14th Annual Symposium of AASWG, edited by Benj. L. Stempler and Marilyn Glass with Christine M. Savinelli

Capturing the Power of Diversity, Selected Proceedings of the 13th Annual Symposium of AASWG, edited by Marvin D. Feit, John H. Ramey, John S. Wodarski, and Aaron R. Mann

Group Work: Skills and Strategies for Effective Interventions by Sondra Brandler and Camille P. Roman

Elements of the Helping Process: A Guide for Clinicians by Raymond Fox

Clinical Social Work Supervision, Second Edition by Carlton E. Munson

Intervention Research: Design and Development for the Human Services edited by Jack Rothman and Edwin J. Thomas

Building on Women's Strengths: A Social Work Agenda for the Twenty-First Century edited by Liane V. Davis

Environmental Practice in the Human Services: Integration of Micro and Macro Roles, Skills, and Contexts by Bernard Neugeboren

Basic Social Policy and Planning: Strategies and Practice Methods by Hobart A. Burch

Social Work Intervention in an Economic Crisis: The River Communities Project by Martha Baum and Pamela Twiss

Feminist Theories and Social Work: Approaches and Applications by Christine Flynn Saulnier

Principles of Social Work Practice: A Generic Practice Approach by Molly R. Hancock

Social Work in Health Settings: Practice in Context, Second Edition by Toba Schwaber Kerson and Associates

From Prevention to Wellness Through Group Work

Joan K. Parry, DSW
Editor

The Haworth Press
New York • London

The Haworth Press, Inc., 10 Alice Street, Binghamton, NY 13904-1580

Cover design by Monica L. Seifert.

Library of Congress Cataloging-in-Publication Data

Parry, Joan K.
    From prevention to wellness through group work / Joan K. Parry.
        p.   cm.
    Includes bibliographical references and index.
    ISBN 0-7890-0164-0 (alk. paper)
    1. Social group work. I. Title.
HV45.P38 1997
361.4–dc21
                                               96-48820
                                                 CIP

CONTENTS

About the Editor   x

Contributors   xi

Preface   xv

**Chapter 1. Constructivism, Power, and Social Work
  with Groups**   1
  Gale Goldberg-Wood
  Ruth R. Middleman

Language   4
Power   5
Practice Implications   6
Multilogue   6
Decision Making/Turntaking   7
Subtle Oppression   10
Consciousness Raising   11
Conclusion   11

**Chapter 2. The Empowerment Group: The Heart
  of the Empowerment Approach and an Antidote
  to Injustice**   15
  Judith A.B. Lee

Introduction   15
The Empowerment Approach As Paradigm   17
Personal and Political Power Are Interrelated   18
Empowerment Theory and Groups   21
The Interactionist Approach and the Mutual-Aid Group   22
Communications and Workers' Roles   23
Critical Education and Conscientization   24
The Empowerment Group Approach   24
Group Examples   24
The "Successful Women's Group"   25
Conclusion   29

Chapter 3. Groups for the Socialization to Old Age   **33**
Margaret E. Betty Hartford
Susan Lawton

Senior Centers   37
Administrative Groups   37
Education, Personal Enhancement, and Support Groups   38
Activity Groups   39
Groups for Senior Participation   40
System Maintenance Groups   42
Service Provision Groups   43
Groups for Providing Social Relationships   44
Personal Growth Groups   44
Conclusion   44

**Chapter 4. Psychoeducational Groups: A Model
for Recovery and Celebration of the Self**   **47**
Carol F. Kuechler

Definition and Model in Context   47
From "Pure" Education to Psychotherapy, Hospitalization,
  and Medication   50
Case Example: Implementation and Evaluation
  of This Model   52
Focus Group Questions   56

**Chapter 5. Conflict Management in Group Treatment:
"Get Out of My Face, You S.O.B.!"**   **61**
Kenneth E. Reid

Defining Conflict   61
Worker Ambivalence   62
Positive Effects of Conflict   63
Personal Conflict-Response Modes   65
Sources of Group Conflict   68
Anger Toward the Leader   69
Conflict Management Strategies   70
Summary   75

Chapter 6. Research and Groups: A Mutual Aid System?   **79**
Alice Home

Enhancing Research Through Group Techniques   79
Using Research to Improve Group Practice   84
Conclusion   87

Chapter 7. Bullying and Scapegoating in Groups:
Process and Interventions   **89**
Hisashi Hirayama
Kasumi Hirayama

Functions of the Scapegoat   91
Interventions   93
Preventing Scapegoating   97
Conclusion   99

Chapter 8. Helping Long-Term Homeless Men Regain
Their Personhood Through Social Group Work   **101**
Janet S. Elder

Background   101
Involvement with Others   101
Developing Skills   104
Increasing Self-Efficacy   105
Developing a Critical Consciousness   106

Chapter 9. Developing Social Skills Programs
for Children with Emotional Disabilities   **109**
Juanita B. Hepler

Importance of Social Interactions   111
Implementation of the Study   112
Summary   119

Chapter 10. Group Work Education and the CSWE
Curriculum Policy Statement: Capitulation
or Coexistence?   **123**
Cyrus S. Behroozi

Transformation of the Curriculum Policy Statement   123
Response to the Curriculum Policy Statement   127
Obstacles to Group-Work Education   129

**Chapter 11. A Self-Directed Community Group
for Homeless People: Poetry in Motion**   131
    Marcia B. Cohen
    Julie M. Johnson

Introduction   131
Background and Organizational Context   132
Structure and Composition   133
Group Purpose and Goals   134
Internal Leadership   136
Community Building Through Poetry   138
The Role of the Worker in Self-Directed Groups   140
Summary   141

**Chapter 12. Social Group Work with the Elderly
Mentally Ill: Beauty in the Beast**   143
    John L. Hart

Poetry in the State Hospital Setting: "Fresh Red
    Strawberries"   143
The Poetry Writers' Workshop Group   144
How to Write a Poem   145
Special Projects   147
Conclusions and Recommendations   147

**Chapter 13. Refiguring Group-Work Services
with People with AIDS**   151
    George S. Getzel

Review of the Literature   152
Clash of Ideologies   152
Design Changes in the 1990s   153
A Comprehensive Group Program   154
Orientation Support Group as Linchpin   155
Conclusion   158

Chapter 14. Post-Transplant Group . . . Five Years On 161
    Joanne Avery

Introduction   161
Background   161

History   161
Importance of Group Support   162
Role of Facilitator   163
Nature of Group Support   165
Membership and Format   166
Supportive Elements and Themes   167
Elements Important to Staff/Group Relationship   168
Preventative Aspects   169
Challenges   170

Index   **173**

ABOUT THE EDITOR

Joan K. Parry, DSW, has 20 years' experience as a social work practitioner and teacher and is Professor Emeritus from the San Jose State University School of Social Work. Dr. Parry served on the five-member National Task Force of the National Association of Social Workers to write continuing education standards for 100,000 professional social workers. She has held numerous other positions in NASW in both the New York and California state chapters and is also a member of the Council on Social Work Education. Dr. Parry is the author of several articles, chapters, and books, including *Social Work Practice with the Terminally Ill* (1989) and *A Cross Cultural Look at Death, Dying, and Religion* (1995).

CONTRIBUTORS

Joanne Avery, BA, BSW, MSW, CSW, is currently a social worker in the Autologous Blood and Marrow Transplant Program at Toronto Hospital, Toronto, Ontario.

Cyrus S. Behroozi, DSW, is a professor of social work at Indiana University, Indianapolis. He has served as chair of the AASWG Chapter Development Committee and as a member of the CSWE Commission on Accreditation. He has presented at many conferences and has published in several journals, including *Social Work with Groups* and *Groupwork.*

Marcia B. Cohen, MSW, PhD, is an associate professor at the University of New England School of Social Work in Biddeford, Maine, where she teaches courses in group work, generalist practice, social welfare policy, and homelessness. Marcia has published extensively in the area of mutual aid and social action groups for homeless people. She is very interested in the role of the group worker in self-directed groups and currently serves on the board of a consumer-run, mental health social club.

Janet S. Elder, MSW, is currently employed at Ten Broeck Hospital in Lyndon, Kentucky as a social worker on the adult unit. Ten Broeck Hospital is an acute-care facility.

George S. Getzel, DSW, is a professor at the Hunter College School of Social Work of the City University of New York, and teaches social group work and chairs the Group Work Sequence. He is a consultant to the Gay Men's Health Crisis, the oldest and largest voluntary agency in the world serving people with AIDS.

Gale Goldberg-Wood, MSW, EdD, is a professor of social work in the Kent School of Social Work, University of Louisville, Kentucky. She has authored and co-authored numerous books and articles dealing with the structural approach to direct practice, skills for work with individuals and groups, perception and cognition, constructivism, power, interpersonal violence, social group work, and teaching in social work education. She has a small private practice and serves on the editorial boards of three journals.

John L. Hart, PhD, BCD, is an associate professor at Alabama A&M University in the Graduate Social Work Program. He is the former chief geropsychiatric social worker at Camarillo State Hospital in California. He is a poet and makes use of poetry in his teaching and training of mental health professionals. His current research interests are groups with men, the National Fathering Project in Norway, and training group workers in Alabama and Norway.

Margaret E. Betty Hartford, AB, MSSA, PhD, is a community volunteer in Claremont, California, working with senior programs including the Committee on Aging. She is a resident of Mt. San Antonio Gardens retirement community, where she chairs the Residents' Health Services Committee. She also serves on the boards of several senior programs, writes a monthly column on successful aging, and teaches a class on transitions to retirement. She is an Emeritus Professor of the University of Southern California in gerontology and social work, and taught group work at Case Western Reserve for 25 years.

Juanita B. Hepler, PhD, is professor and director of the MSW Program in the School of Social Work at Boise State University. Her research interests have focused on families and children, with a special emphasis on the social development of children and the implementation and evaluation of social skills programs.

Hisashi Hirayama, DSW, is the associate dean/director and a professor at the University of Tennessee, Knoxville, College of Social Work.

Kasumi Hirayama, DSW, is an associate professor at the University of Connecticut, School of Social Work, in West Hartford, CT.

Alice Home, MSW, PhD, is a professor of social work at Ecole de Service Social, University of Ottawa, Canada, where she teaches group work and research methods. She has also taught intercultural practice, preventive methods, women and social work, and community work. While her current teaching is entirely at the graduate level, she has also taught undergraduates at the University of Montreal and Laval University. Her main group work interests are women's groups focused on empowerment, and she has done extensive research on women's issues.

Julie M. Johnson is the Street Outreach Case Manager at Holy Innocents in Portland, Maine. She is also a graduate student at the University of New England in Biddeford, Maine. She has cofacilitated political action groups with people who attended a homeless drop-in center in Portland, Maine.

Carol F. Kuechler, PhD, is an assistant professor in the School of Social Work at the College of St. Catherine/University of St. Thomas. Her interests include group work, supervision/consultation, and research.

Susan Lawton, BA, has worked in social services for over 14 years, the last seven of which have been as a supervisor of senior citizen programs for the City of Claremont, California. She has completed course work for an MSW degree and will finish her thesis in 1996.

Judith A. B. Lee, DSW, is a professor of social work at the University of Connecticut School of Social Work and chair of the Casework Sequence. She has also taught at Columbia University and New York University and was chair of the Group Work Sequence at NYU. She is the past president of AASWG. Also she is the author of *The Empowerment Approach to Social Work Practice* (1994) and the editor of *Group Work with the Poor and Oppressed* (1989).

Ruth R. Middleman, EdD, is Professor Emerita in the Raymond A. Kent School of Social Work, University of Louisville, Kentucky. She is the author of many books and multiple articles in all known social work journals and other journals.

Kenneth E. Reid, PhD, ACSW, is a professor in the School of Social Work at Western Michigan University in Kalamazoo, Michigan. He teaches group work in the graduate program and regularly leads groups in the community.

Preface

This book represents the most advanced thinking and practice in the arena of social work with groups. There are two plenary papers in this volume: Chapter 1 from Ruth Middleman and Gale Goldberg-Wood and Chapter 2 from Judith A. B. Lee. Middleman and Wood present new ideas and theory using the constructivism and power model. Lee elaborates on the empowerment theme. The remaining 12 chapters in this book represent a mix of academics and practice authors. These authors provide chapters that describe practices in both Canada and in the United States, where the authors reside in the West, the Midwest, the South, and the East. The subjects vary, including conflict management, research in groups, socialization to old age, poetry groups in a mental hospital for the elderly, a social skills program for emotionally disturbed children, bullying and scapegoating in groups, groups for patients who have experienced transplants, and groups for people with AIDS.

This book will enable social group workers in the United States, Canada, and around the world to read about the new and interesting ideas presented at the 1995 Annual Symposium of the Association for the Advancement of Social Work with Groups in San Diego, California.

Chapter 1

Constructivism, Power, and Social Work with Groups

Gale Goldberg-Wood
Ruth R. Middleman

The title of this chapter, "Constructivism, Power, and Social Work with Groups," is a mouthful. Constructivism–how one interprets, or makes sense of the world–and the dynamics of power–how persons replicate in the small group the power relations that go on elsewhere, in other contexts–are two sets of ideas that, when taken together, have important implications for doing social work with groups.

Consider constructivism through the following illustration:

> Chicken Little thought the sky was falling. A piece of it had landed on her head. And she quickly went to inform Goosey-Lucy, Henny-Penny, Ducky-Lucky, Turkey-Lurkey and her other friends in the barnyard. She wanted to warn them; to tell them they should run for their lives. (Kellogg, 1985)

This was Chicken Little's reality; this is what she knew. If we had been there, we might have seen that what fell on her head was an acorn. Our reality would have been different from hers. As well, had there been a giggling child with a pea shooter high up in the branches of a tree and proud of his aim, his reality might have been different from Chicken Little's and from ours. There are many realities. The view depends not merely on the point of view, but on the point of *viewer*. Ideas of this sort are gaining acceptance across many disciplines under the rubric *constructivism*.

1

Constructivism suggests that all persons make their own realities. Even twins create different realities unique to each. These realities spring from what people have experienced and become the screens through which they see the world–their perspectives, their frames of reference. One's perspective provides a general orientation of prearranged ideas, attitudes, and expectations that keep one's world in order. It determines what has meaning and value, how much openness and difference one can entertain, and what must be ignored or transformed because it does not fit with one's expectations and system of beliefs. So constructivism has implications for the understanding derived by group workers of group participants' communications with each other as well as with themselves. It affects the practitioner's thoughts about what is going on in the world of the group.

Constructivism puts the self of the constructor into all that she or he sees and experiences. It says something about the *how* of perception and about the constructor's frame of reference–other concepts that have been used to explore matters of thinking. It is an epistemology, an approach to considering how one knows what one knows, by what means one knows it, and also what counts as real knowledge. For example, in Japan, many businessmen now reserve the term *knowledge* for only hunches, skills, and insights. The rest they consider mere information (*The Economist*, 1995). People in the United States still see and value information as important knowledge, as many introductory courses in academia reveal.

Meaning and how one translates seeing and experiencing into knowing is at the heart of constructivism. But we do not see through pristine eyes. The lenses of our eyes are smudged with history, spotted with personal and cultural experience, and some of our lenses are deeply scarred by our subordinate status in the socio-political realm (Swigonski, 1993). This applies not only to people of color and the elderly in a white, youth-valuing patriarchy, but can also be applied to social work among the professions, and to group work within social work. Again, the view depends not merely on the point of view, but on the point of the *viewer*. Interpretation, or the meaning given to perceived events, comes from the "I" behind the eye. And that "I" has been misled by many forces. Certain things are remembered, others are forgotten. Davies (1995), an historian, describes several categories of selectivity that affect what we think we "know":

- Propaganda–the deliberate techniques of emphasizing only particular "facts"
- Geographical selectivity or parochialism–the way in which national self-interest determines the report of events (for example, the history of war as written by the victors)
- Stereotypes–the lumping together of varieties of individuals and describing them collectively, usually negatively
- Selective statistics–the use of numbers that will support one's favored perspective over others'
- Professionals' biases–the way different specialties or theories direct diverse conclusions
- Moral selectivity–the promotion of programs or actions that justify what one believes is "good"

Davies cautioned that selectivity is unavoidable, and one should admit this to oneself. Constructivism helps us own our human limitations and reminds us that we all call our own biased seeing and knowing "reality," as if there are no alternate realities with as much credence as our own. We must learn that there are many realities, and that nothing is as certain as we think it is. Nothing is as certain as uncertainty.

Yet, as has been stated in social work literature, ". . . clinicians often assume a stance of certainty . . . a belief that they actually know what a client is experiencing in the particular context of his or her life" (Pozatek, 1994, p. 396). No doubt they do this under the constant pressure to make judgments and act on them. This pressure is even greater for persons who work with groups, since there are so many realities at work in any group session! It has been said that convergence of these multiple realities enables group formation (Shapiro, 1990), but the process is dauntingly complex; while learning may take place, and ways to make multiperspectival decisions can be created and used to advantage for all, convergence is at best approximate.

An event becomes an experience when it is given meaning and therefore interpretation. Meaning is confirmed, confounded, contradicted, or compromised through talk with others. This is how social reality is created. One's known reality arises through participation in a family, group, neighborhood, school, church, workplace–that is, through one's culture. It is perpetuated and extended by the ubiquitous, conspicuous media of today's world. In all instances there is a group exerting influence on its members' beliefs about what is real. Social reality is actively created and perpetuated in groups, and it is more subtly influenced by movies, television programming, advertizing, computer games, the Internet, and most especially, by one's language.

LANGUAGE

We express our ideas through language. At the same time, our language limits what we can think about, how we can think about it, and what we can say to each other. Common sense might suggest that people thought up different words in order to express their ideas about the world and about themselves in it. However, 40 years ago the great contribution of the linguist Benjamin Whorf (1956) was the insight that the language we have at our command influences the very thoughts we can have, and thus the actions we can take.

From his extensive study of American Indian tongues, Whorf concluded that speakers of a language agree to perceive and think about the world in a certain way, though not the only possible way. This pertains to professional language with its special jargon as well. Each language embodies and perpetuates a particular culture's worldview and determines the kinds of thoughts people of that culture can entertain. For example, our country thinks a lot about war. Its influence is insidious, pervasive, and unrelenting. As a result, our language has a lot of war-related words. Consider the following: the Salvation Army, the Peace Corps, the Childrens' Defense Fund; we battle discrimination, kill a bill, attack problems, fight AIDS, deploy personpower, wipe out, conquer, combat, zero in on, induct, debrief, and discharge. In other cultures, such as Japan, the concept of war is greatly muted, a concept not available for use in thinking.

In *The Power of Words*, Chase (cited in Hayakawa, 1963) claims that our Indo-European language heritage produces a two-valued orientation: this or that, right or wrong, good or bad, which leads us to think in dichotomies. Something either is or is not, with little room for ranges of "is-ness." Such dichotomous thinking, by relying on contrasts, obscures ambiguity as well as intermediate possibilities, and thereby limits understanding and other possible action (Berlin, 1990). Language, with its powerful limitations on thinking, complicates efforts to exchange ideas and makes it even harder for people to understand each other's realities. Efforts to understand difference have always been a familiar challenge to those who work with groups–whether the difference is class, race, age, or gender.

POWER

It is power that determines what is real and attended to, what is emphasized rather than discounted, and what is ultimately silenced and ignored. "What is taken for 'the truth' depends primarily on social factors such as power, social negotiation and prestige" (Gergen, 1991, p. 93). Constructivism can shed light on power and its ramifications.

According to Breton (1994), power is the right to say and have a say. Power is also the right to categorize and name things, to "call the shots" (Luepnitz, 1988). Power is having the political and economic clout to promote one's own preferred version of reality, the version of reality that benefits and keeps those in power in power. They get to decide, for example, what children are taught in the schools and what they are not taught; or what is and is not preached from the pulpits. Power is distributed by social class and guarded by like-minded class-*mates.* And according to *Newsweek* (1995), a new class seems to be emerging with its own values and preferences–a monied, merit-oriented *overclass*, rapidly drawing in yesteryear's Yuppies. *Newsweek*, by naming the overclass, confirms it as a reality.

Power also involves the creation of specialized disciplines and practices, each with its regime of power and truth within which matters of what is acceptable and what is extraneous are determined (Foucault, 1980). Those who control what counts as knowledge, such as journal editors, are a good example. As a recent editor of *Social Work* said,

> . . . every time an article is accepted or rejected, the editors
> make an epistemological decision that not only is part of the

process of defining the profession and its truth, but also has
political implications in the distribution of intellectual leadership, power and status . . . (Hartman, 1990, p. 3)

Let us note that there is rarely an article on group work in *Social
Work*. Perhaps this precipitated the creation of our journal, *Social
Work with Groups,* and perhaps helped precipitate the Association
for the Advancement of Social Work with Groups (AASWG) itself,
and the yearly Symposia—three places where our professional
voices could be expressed. In this organization, as well, journal
editors and Symposia sponsors determine whose group work matters and should be promulgated and whose will be ignored; that is,
who will be the intellectual leaders in group work.

Power is present in all social living. It is inequitably distributed
such that some have more power than others. This is true both
outside and inside the group. Power becomes an issue for groups
when oppressive behavior learned outside the group is used inside
the group, and when new and different ways of thinking and being,
created through the group process, are maintained and even spread
outside the group.

PRACTICE IMPLICATIONS

Four ideas for practice emerge from understanding aspects of
constructivism and some of the dynamics of power: (1) multilogue,
(2) turntaking as a technique for decision making, (3) subtle oppression in the group, and (4) the need for consciousness raising.

MULTILOGUE

Dialogue is a very familiar concept these days. Careful attention
to the original meaning of the term "dialogue" however, reveals its
two-person nature. For group work, we propose the concept *multilogue*. Multilogue, unlike dialogue, involves many people. It is a
process, attended to by the worker, through which group members
develop shared meanings. Through multilogue, group participants

talk to each other about how to understand events that occur in the group and elsewhere, and how to react to them. They do this primarily through talking; however, there is nonverbal agreement and disagreement as well. Through the multilogue process, multiple, individual meanings merge, forming the socially constructed realities of that particular group. This is what makes groups powerful. Through multilogue, groups define a social reality, and therefore the meaning of experience, by developing group norms regarding how particular events are to be construed and by expecting adherence to those norms. One reason support groups are so successful is because people *believe* and are encouraged to believe in their created, shared realities.

Multilogue involves contributions from virtually everyone present. It is not a serial dialogue between the worker and individual members while the rest look on. This latter communication pattern is what Kurland and Salmon (1992) refer to as *casework in a group* rather than group work. To be called group work, the primary interaction ought to be among the members.

In discussing and determining what is happening in the group, some participants speak louder than others. Some talk more often than others. Some are quiet. It is a challenge to the worker to facilitate the expressiveness of the whole group. This is best accomplished by encouraging as many persons as possible to have their say, despite the presence of dominant persons. This is especially important since we live in a cultural environment that encourages survival of the loudest. Dominance prevails if not deliberately interrupted, and the worker who supports and encourages *multilogue* is more likely to interrupt dominant voices, to tune in on the pulse of the whole group, and to be less likely to dominate the group.

DECISION MAKING/TURNTAKING

Through multilogue, the business of the small, face-to-face group is transacted. A crucial part of these transactions involves decision making. The most common way that groups make decisions is by voting and majority rule. This form of decision making is learned in the culture-at-large and is then transported into the small group. Sometimes, however, such know-how is not used. Gitterman's (1989) work with a group of teens is illustrative. Chaos prevailed in the group until he introduced a three-part communication and decision-making structure: round robin to get the ideas out, group discussion of the ideas, then voting.

Even though majority rule and voting are the primary ways for making decisions in our culture, there are problems with them. First of all, majority rule results in winners and losers. As with all winnings and losings, no one wants to lose. Secondly, over time, use of voting can result in a *consistent* majority ruling and a consistent minority losing, a situation vulnerable to tyranny by the majority.

Lani Guinier (1994) describes an interesting discussion about voting that she had with her four-year-old son, Nikolas:

> [Our discussion was] prompted by a *Sesame Street Magazine* exercise. The magazine pictured six children: four children had raised their hands because they wanted to play tag; two had their hands down because they wanted to play hide-and-seek. The magazine asked its readers to count the number of children whose hands were raised and then decide what game the children would play. [Nikolas had a ready answer.] "They will play both. First they will play tag. Then they will play hide-and-seek." Despite the magazine's "rules," he was right . . . The winner may get to play first or more often, but even the loser gets something . . . fair play means that the rules encourage everyone to play. They [the rules] should reward those who win, but they must be acceptable to those who lose. (pp. 1-2)

In game-theory terms, decision making does not have to be a zero-sum enterprise. Rather it could be a win-win situation.

In addition to decision making by voting and majority rule, there is decision making by consensus, a process in which participants talk with each other until they come to a unanimous choice after some have been willing to modify their own ideas. However, the demand for conformity is great, and sometimes if some, even one participant, is unwilling to compromise, there is much frustration and no decision reached. Thus, consensus is vulnerable to becoming tyranny by the minority.

We propose a third decision-making alternative: *turntaking*. Turntaking is familiar to adults who stand in bakery and supermarket lines, and who wait their turns to pay bridge tolls. Turntaking is most commonly associated with the doing of shared activities. If one watches children on the playground, one can see that taking turns is hard learned—there are power differences in terms of size, gender, age. Games are a major way in which children learn to take turns: consider starters such as *Candyland* and *Chutes and Ladders*, then jacks, hopscotch, and Little League baseball. Berman-Rossi and Cohen (1988) discuss a dinner group for homeless, mentally ill adult, female residents of a single-room occupancy hotel: "The creation of activities through which social relationships could develop was the charge . . ." (Berman-Rossi and Cohen, 1988, p. 68), and over a five-year period, their group developed around tasks such as planning a menu, developing a shopping list, shopping, managing a budget, preparing the meal, eating, and cleaning up. In their discussion, they refer to turntaking in terms of task rotation for accomplishing these necessary chores—again, turntaking in the doing of activities.

Turntaking is also a communication format (Middleman and Goldberg-Wood, 1990, p. 106). Round robin, used by Gitterman (1989) with the teens, is common for introductions of participants to each other. Duffy (1994) provides an extensive review of the literature on turntaking as a communication structure, variously labeled check-ins, go-rounds, and round robins. Go-rounds are sometimes used to accelerate and compact the group process. They are used in the first meeting of a group; they are used as opening or closing rituals; they are used with particular populations to develop specific coping skills; they are used to get feedback and to take a quick poll on issues. While go-rounds can be a helpful communication structure in particular circumstances, Duffy cautions against their routine use because they interfere with member-to-member communication and the natural development of the group. Another use of turntaking as a communication structure is found in therapy groups where members claim time to work.

Turntaking for decision making is a little-known mechanism with considerable possibilities. While it is not an emphasized part of our culture, it can be used to advantage in group work. Often, we vote or try for consensus when it is not necessary. If there is more than one choice, perhaps all can happen—on different days or during different parts of the same day. Instead of either/or thinking, it can be this-and-that thinking; win-win instead of zero-sum. For example, teenagers in residential facilities can take turns choosing what the group does on Saturday night. In a group that has speakers, instead of voting on each speaker, each member can choose one person to speak. In any hobby or interest group, members can take turns determining the focus for the day. Elder (1995) reports that in her group of homeless, alcoholic men, each man, in turn, got to plan the activities that all did on consecutive weeks. Among other things, this group took a trip to Wal-Mart, went fossil hunting, drove through the park, saw a baseball game, and had a cookout. Their interests in and commitments to the whole group experience increased.

Turntaking is much more than power sharing on the part of the worker, although this does happen. The key with the homeless men is the responsibility each man held and felt for a given meeting. This responsibility gave a message for cooperation to the men, as well as a sense of ownership to the originator of each plan. Turntaking can empower group members. This holds for the homeless men as well as for all of the other examples. The very history of the AASWG Symposia demonstrates the workings of turntaking–starting with Cleveland and then moving annually to 16 other cities in the United States and Canada.

SUBTLE OPPRESSION

One kind of event that occurs in a small group, which participants can try to understand and determine how to react to through multilogue, is oppression. As part of their perspectives (their frames of reference) people bring into the group the power and status relations that exist outside the group because they are built into the culture and the culture socializes its members to maintain them. Brown and Mistry (1994) specifically hone in on race and gender, as being two powerful determinants of one's worldview as well as being major reference points for status and therefore oppression, right there in the group. They contend, and we agree, that while sensitivity is necessary, it is not a sufficient response to oppressions in a mixed-race and/or mixed-gender social work group. Brown and Mistry state that the worker should "intervene in a way which is strong and unequivocal . . . [and] expose [the] oppressive behavior, [albeit] in a way which is not so confrontive that it creates a defensive reinforcing reaction" (Brown and Mistry, 1994, p. 18). It should be clear enough for oppressive behavior to become content for group discussion. When the worker observes an oppressive behavior happening in the group, she or he should call attention to it and encourage full discussion of it.

CONSCIOUSNESS RAISING

Consciousness raising involves learning that one's own negative personal experiences and the consistently debasing ways in which one has been and continues to be treated by others is not due to one's personal deficits or limits. Rather, one learns that such unfair treatment and the consequences of it have been and continue to be endured by a whole category of people who share one's devalued, ascribed characteristics (e.g., African Americans and women). Consciousness raising can profoundly alter one's perspective.

As we have written elsewhere, ". . . the group is known to be the ideal medium for consciousness raising. It is an intimate and mutually supportive situation for discussion of lived trauma, for examination of the relationship between experience and political ascription, and for subsequent social action" (Middleman and Goldberg-Wood, 1995, p. 11). Recognition that one's self is not deficient nor held down by personal shortcomings can reduce the quest for self-help books as solutions to one's struggles and can increase the likelihood of engagement with others in political and social action to change the situation.

CONCLUSION

Constructivism affects one's practice. Regardless of the theoretical orientation used in working with a group, the practitioner's interpretation of what is going on affects what is actually occurring. This is a powerful and sobering claim. It is sobering because it suggests how very powerful even a seemingly benign practitioner actually is, and how careful the worker must be to deliberately encompass the group's knowings. The power of language has also been noted: how the words we have at our command limit the very thoughts we are able to form.

While it is not radically new to say that people see things differently, nor that their points of view differ, what *is* different is the central emphasis that people actively make their own realities. They construct them out of the totality of their lives: out of their lore, their traditions and other learnings, out of their values and spiritual beliefs. And these are their realities, the screens through which they see their worlds. Hopefully, workers will be mindful that there are many possible realities.

Perhaps the word *multilogue* will become part of every group worker's vocabulary and will be central in her or his thinking. Once this happens, the practitioner will be more likely to focus on member-to-member talk, on helping members try to understand each other's talk and each other's meanings. There will be conditional differences such as age, gender, and social class. Teens, for example, may want to think the same way their friends think; conformity may be essential. Then there may be times when asserting one's difference, one's uniqueness, one's separate identity is a central goal. These differences, too, must be factored in by the practitioner. Furthermore, thinking *multilogue* signals practitioners to be suspicious if the main voices they hear are their own (Middleman and Goldberg-Wood, 1995).

The idea of turntaking was introduced as a decision-making technique that acknowledges in action the diversity that constructivist insights require. Turntaking is a response to worker understanding that there are many realities at work in the group. This is especially important in mixed-race/mixed-gender groups and in groups where consciousness raising is imperative. Turntaking pushes toward involvement of all in determining the destiny of the group.

REFERENCES

Berlin, S. (1990). Dichotomous and complex thinking. *Social Service Review*, 64(1):46-59.

Berman-Rossi, T. and Cohen, M. (1988). Group development and shared decision-making working with homeless, mentally ill women. *Social Work with Groups*, 11(4):63-78.

Breton, M. (1994). On the meaning of empowerment and empowerment-oriented social work practice. *Social Work with Groups*, 17(3):23-37.

Brown, A. and Mistry, T. (1994). Group work with "mixed membership" groups: Issues of race and gender. *Social Work with Groups,* 17(3):5-21.

Davies, N. (1995). The misunderstood Europe. *New York Review,* XLII, 9, 7-11.

Duffy, T. (1994). The check-in and other go-rounds: Guidelines for use. *Social Work with Groups,* 17(1/2):163-175.

In praise of knowledge. *The Economist* (1995). May 27, p. 20.

Elder, J. (1995). Helping long-term homeless men regain their personhood through social group work. Paper presented at the 17th Annual International Symposium on Social Work with Groups, San Diego, California, October.

Elder, Jerry. The rise of the overclass. *Newsweek* (1995), July 31, pp. 32-33.

Foucault, M. (1980). *Power/Knowledge.* New York: Pantheon.

Gergen, K. (1991). *The Saturated Self.* New York: Basic Books.

Gitterman, A. (1989). Building mutual support in groups. *Social Work with Groups,* 12(2):5-21.

Guinier, L. (1994). *The Tyranny of the Majority.* New York: Free Press.

Hartman, A. (1990). Many ways of knowing. *Social Work,* 35(1):3-4.

Hayakawa, S.I. (1963). *Language in Thought and Action* (Second Edition). New York: Harcourt, Brace & World.

Kellogg, S. (1985). *Chicken Little Retold and Illustrated.* New York: William Morrow.

Kurland, R. and Salmon, R. (1992). Group work vs. casework in a group: Implications for teaching and practice. *Social Work with Groups,* 15(4):3-14.

Luepnitz, D. (1988). Bateson's heritage: Bitter fruit. *The Family Therapist Networker,* September/October:49.

Middleman, R. and Goldberg-Wood, G. (1990). *Skills for Direct Practice in Social Work.* New York: Columbia University Press, p. 106.

Middleman, R. and Goldberg-Wood, G. (1995). Contextual group work: Apprehending the elusive obvious. In R. Kurland and R. Salmon, *Group Work Practice in a Troubled Society.* Binghamton, NY: The Haworth Press, Inc., pp. 5-17.

Pozatek, E. (1994). The problem of certainty: Clinical social work in the postmodern era. *Social Work,* 39:(4):396-403.

Shapiro, B. (1990). The social work group as social microcosm: "Frames of reference" revisited. *Social Work with Groups,* 13(2):5-21.

Swigonski, M. (1993). Feminist standpoint theory and the question of social work research. *Affilia,* 8(2):171-183.

Whorf, B. (1956). *Language, Thought and Reality.* New York: Wiley.

Chapter 2

The Empowerment Group:
The Heart of the Empowerment Approach
and an Antidote to Injustice

Judith A. B. Lee

INTRODUCTION

This symposium, AASWG's seventeenth, promises to expand the foundation of social-work thinking and practice with groups from prevention to the wellness of people and societies as we approach the twenty-first century. For many, the burgeoning of new technologies and the possibility of creating a global village promotes excitement and optimism. Yet social workers experience hope, anxiety, and outrage for we must stop and say, "Wait a minute, there is something wrong with this picture." All of this wonderful new technology and people are still poor! *People are still poor:* in resources, in body, in mind, and in spirit. People are still victimized, economically as well as physically. Minority groups are bitterly divided against each other. Oppression and discrimination may be stronger than ever. Barometric events in Los Angeles, including the 1992 mass rioting after the Rodney King verdict (where West [1993] notes only 36 percent of those arrested were African American, as race was only a catalyst for generalized unhappiness among low-income Americans); the 1994-1995 Simpson trial; and similar backdrops for the drama of antagonism throughout the country have made us painfully aware of the hold racism, anti-Semitism, sexism, and all the other "isms" have on our society. Violence, whether institutionalized or bottom-up, begets violence. This is a society that must remove the cancer of hate and meanspiritedness, and heal.

Yet forecasters who predicted that the year 2000 would bring a "kinder, gentler, more equal America" are, so far, mistaken. In the 1980s, during the Reagan-Bush era, it was a time when the rich and super-rich got richer at the expense of all others. The Republican majority has now launched a reactionary revolution that falls only a little short (hopefully by the power of the President's veto) of reversing the minimal social programs established during the New Deal. Medicaid and Medicare, school lunch, Aid to Families with Dependent Children, Child Welfare Services, daycare, and mental and physical health services lie in the balance. In the first 100 days of the "Contract with America," nine regressive measures were passed, including tax cuts for the rich (*Hartford Courant*, April 8, 1995:1, A8), all disproportionately affecting the poor and all historically oppressed groups, especially children and legal immigrants (*Hartford Courant*, March 25, 1995:1, A9). To quote House minority leader Richard Gephardt, the "contract" did not create even a single job: "Never has so much been done, in so little time, to help so few, at the expense of so many . . . The first hundred days have been for the privileged" (*Hartford Courant*, April 8, 1995:A8). So, also, have the hundreds of days after. The word "reform" has become a code word for destruction. With such "reform," access to resources will be determined by geography (*Hartford Courant*, October 1, 1995:A3). Social services will be driven by managed-care interests, and research and theory will be developed to fit insurance companies' policies.

President Clinton's "Covenant with America" is highly compromised. Where then is the hope of the working class, the middle class, and the poor? The hope is, I submit, where it has always been—in the hands of the people. This is a vision expressed early in social-work history by such group-work-oriented leaders as Jane Addams (1910); Grace Coyle (1930); and Marjorie Witt Johnson, Coyle's student, an African-American woman, who wrote her Master's thesis on empowerment through the arts in 1938 (Lee, 1994; Simon, 1994).

Sociopolitical conflict, economic hardship, and the uneven distribution of resources are a problem all over the world. Homelessness in the United States is prototypic of poverty in the midst of affluence. Advocates for the homeless estimate about three million are homeless on any given night in the United States. Almost 50 percent of African-American and Hispanic children are born into poverty, and over 10 percent of all Americans live in poverty (Lee, 1994). Yet poverty in industrialized nations cannot be compared to the abject poverty of many developing countries.

THE EMPOWERMENT APPROACH AS PARADIGM

I see the empowerment approach as a paradigm for international social work practice. A paradigm serves as a pattern, a universal exemplar, a model, or an archetype (*Oxford English Dictionary*, 1971). While the empowerment approach will be refined by each one who practices it, its basic structure specifies the ingredients needed to practice with poor and oppressed groups beyond national boundaries. It relates to individual as well as sociopolitical and economic development in the face of human oppression. Richard Estes, speaking at the twelfth AASWG symposium, noted that there are six types of social development/liberation practice: personal empowerment, group empowerment, conflict resolution, institution building, nation building, and world building (Estes, 1991). Consciousness raising, empowering group process, and the process of praxis–action-reflection-action–are the core processes of the empowerment approach *and* of conscientization and social development practice (Estes, 1991; Lee, 1994). Conscientization is also the dominant approach to social work practice throughout Latin America where liberation theology and critical education are primary in the knowledge base of the profession.

The empowerment approach addresses social work's role and function in the midst of worldwide human rights violations and lack of provision for basic human needs such as food, shelter, and safety. In addition to severe poverty, victimization of many types–especially violence against women–is a worldwide problem that occurs in every stratum of society. Battered women constitute 40 percent of homeless families in New York. Worldwatch Institute found the number-one problem shared by women in villages around the world to be "my husband beats me" (EWAR Project, 1992). Women in many countries now have safe places to go to, in the form of battered women's shelters. The group is the "treatment of choice" for both victims and perpetrators of violence, for the oppressed and those who oppress or permit oppression.

The empowerment approach is specifically directed to practice with oppressed groups. The conceptual framework proposes professional purpose, values, principles, knowledge base, and methodology to working with individuals, families, small groups, and communities that face poverty and oppression (Lee, 1994). At the base is the belief that people can join together to affirm life and promote social justice and equal opportunity for all.

Empowerment practice asserts that it is unethical to "treat" victims clinically or interpersonally without attempting to help them raise consciousness, throw the oppressor off their backs, and become victors. Forrest E. Harris, Sr., a leading African-American theologian, notes that oppressed people who have not raised their consciousness "have been victimized by their powerlessness and fear and their translation of these into internal appropriation of subservient and menial roles. [They] turn their frustration inward, destroying themselves and each other . . ." (Harris, 1993). In turn, they face further retribution by the dominant society. Gang violence and many other forms of violence have root in internalized oppression and blocked opportunities, as does the high rate of suicide among minority-of-color youths (West, 1993). Harris (1993) concludes that helping professionals in a time of social crisis must address themselves to both the inner *and* outer liberation of persons. The group, with its potential for human connection, caring and mutual aid, democratic processes, education, and inspiration to social action, is the optimum medium for such empowerment practice. As such, it is an antidote for injustice in these terrible times for poor and working people. Social work practice for the twenty-first century must be personal and political, and group work must be central in this effort.

PERSONAL AND POLITICAL POWER ARE INTERRELATED

The empowerment approach seeks to channel personal/clinical/interpersonal practice and political/social change/activism practice into one mighty flow. Personal and political power are interrelated.

Barbara B. Solomon (1976) was the first to develop the concept of empowerment for the social work profession. She identifies direct and indirect internalized blocks to power. Powerlessness, or the lack of empowerment of individuals, is based on several factors including compromised personal and interpersonal strengths and resources; economic insecurity; absence of experience in the political arena; lack of access to information; lack of training in critical and abstract thought; physical and emotional stress; learned helplessness; and the aspects of a person's emotional or intellectual makeup that prevent him or her from actualizing possibilities that do exist (Cox, 1989). The actual and perceived ability to use resources contributes to a sense of power that is directly connected to self-esteem (Parsons, 1989). Victim blaming can be blatant or subtle as in the concept of codependency so popular today within the helping professions (Ryan, 1971).

Empowerment "deals with a particular kind of block to problem-solving: that imposed by the external society by virtue of a stigmatized collective identity" (Solomon, 1976:21). Empowerment is the process of gaining power, developing power, taking or seizing power, or facilitating or enabling power (Parsons, 1991). Barbara Levy Simon, who has documented the empowerment tradition in social work practice (1994), stresses,

> Empowerment is a reflexive activity, a process capable of being initiated and sustained only by (those) who seek power or self-determination. Others can only aid and abet in this empowerment process.

The empowerment process resides in the person, not the helper. One of the central principles of the empowerment approach is that "people empower themselves, social workers should assist" (identified as Principle 3; Lee, 1994). There are three interlocking dimensions of empowerment: (1) the development of a more positive and potent sense of self; (2) the construction of knowledge and capacity for more critical comprehension of the web of social and political realities of one's environment; and (3) the cultivation of resources and strategies, or more functional competence, for attainment of personal and collective social goals.

Mancoske and Hunzeker define empowerment as "using interventions which enable those with whom we interact to be more in control of the interactions in exchanges . . ." (1989:14, 15). They state that Germain and Gitterman's life model of social-work practice (1980) fits well with an empowerment approach because it allows multilevel examinations and interventions that may be clinical or political and it is almost by definition a praxis model (Mancoske and Hunzeker, 1989). The assessment and interventive methods used in the empowerment approach incorporate the categories and the spirit of the life model and build on them. Both approaches blend group work and individual, community, and political work into a whole. Power also comes from healthy personality development in the face of oppression, which fuels the ability to influence others in the development of self-esteem/identity, self direction, and competence and interpersonal relatedness. Transformation, or throwing off oppression in personal and community life, occurs as people are empowered through consciousness raising, clinical work, and political work to see and reach for alternatives (Harris, 1993). It requires anger toward injustice, the dehumanization of poverty, negative valuations, and the culture of personal greed (Mancoske and Hunzeker, 1989). The strengths perspective of Saleebey (1992) and the structural approach of group workers and holistic theorists Gale Goldberg-Wood and Ruth Middleman (1989) are highly compatible with the empowerment approach. Their later work includes a strong section on group work. They emphasize that social workers must be prepared to "do what needs to be done" (1989) with and for clients. Helen Northen's (1994) clinical social work approach blends individual and group knowledge and skills with special sensitivity to oppression. Lawrence Shulman (1992), Ruth Parsons (1991), Enid Cox (1989), and many others have also incorporated oppression as an important concept in their thinking about groups and social work practice.

Social-work practice must decide whether it will take an option for work with the oppressed, which builds on community and not on self-interest and broadens the possibility of the imaginable as it goes beyond immediate problem solving to the promulgation of hope (Mancoske and Hunzeker, 1989). Two conditions are needed for empowerment: a worker with a raised consciousness and relevant knowledge and skills, and a client who seeks to be empowered.

Powerlessness is low social attractiveness due to poor resources (material resources and knowledge) (Staub-Bernasconi, 1991). To help empower, we must first learn to speak openly with clients about power, then engage in an examination of power bases and strategize how to equalize power. Lorraine Gutiérrez cites consciousness raising as goal, process, and outcome in empowerment work (Gutiérrez, 1990; Gutiérrez and Ortega, 1989). Developing a sense of personal power and skills and working toward social change are the goals of empowerment practice. She sees developing critical consciousness, reducing self-blame, assuming personal responsibility for change, and enhancing self-efficacy as critical to empowerment (Gutiérrez, 1990). Gutiérrez defines group work as central to empowerment practice based on research on the empowering use of ethnic identity and consciousness raising groups with Latino college students and with women of color (Gutiérrez and Ortega, 1989; Gutiérrez, 1990).

EMPOWERMENT THEORY AND GROUPS

Empowerment theory applied to group work was first introduced in 1983 by Ruby B. Pernell in a rousing keynote speech at the fifth annual symposium of AASWG. She said that group work is a natural vehicle for empowerment:

> Empowerment as a goal is a political position, as it challenges the status quo and attempts to change existing power relationships . . . It goes beyond "enabling." It requires of the worker the ability to analyze social processes and interpersonal behavior in terms of power and powerlessness . . . and . . . to enable group members to . . . develop skills in using their influence effectively. (1986:111)

The skills of working with indigenous leadership; knowing resources (where the power lies and how to get it); facilitating cultural-pride activities; utilizing conflict-resolution skills; and enabling the group members to do for themselves are important in attaining empowerment. Ben-Zion Shapiro of Canada notes,

The recent work of Hirayama and Hirayama (1986), Pernell (1986), Lee (1986), Wood and Middleman (1989), Lewis (1989), and Breton (1989a,b) using the language of competence, consciousness-raising and empowerment, is suggestive of theory which goes beyond the conceptualizations of the "social goals" model and its proponents. (1991:16)

The empowerment approach is ground-breaking theory that embraces both personal and political change. The empowerment approach (Lee, 1994) suggests that workers use lenses with five foci "ground in" to see practice with members of oppressed groups: (1) an historical view of the group's oppression; (2) an ecological perspective, including how people cope; (3) ethnic sensitivity; (4) a feminist perspective that appreciates unity, conceptualizations, and the personal as political; and (5) a critical view that challenges structural inequity.

Community is a very important concept in empowerment work. Both Margot Breton (1992) of Canada and Elizabeth Lewis (1991) of the United States have been major contributors in integrating humanism, liberation theology, community group work, and coalition building into empowerment practice. Groups that seek change in the environment are empowering to the degree that group members (not organizers) have actually brought about and reflected upon the change. According to Lewis (1991), face-to-face "grassroots" adult community groups bridge an "interstitial area" between group work and community organization practice. Political empowerment is the purpose, but personal satisfaction, growth, community or ethnic pride, and heightened self-esteem may be byproducts of these experiences.

THE INTERACTIONIST APPROACH
AND THE MUTUAL-AID GROUP

The interactionist approach of master group-work theorist William Schwartz (1974) is a major stepping stone to the empowerment approach. Gitterman and Shulman use the interactionist approach in their work on mutual-aid groups, vulnerable populations, and the life cycle, as well as in their separate theoretical works (Gitterman and Shulman, 1994; Shulman, 1992; and Germain and Gitterman, 1980 and 1996). They see the group as a microcosm of social interaction. The worker's role is to "mediate the processes through which individuals and their systems reach out to each other," particularly when there are obstacles in these transactions—"when the ties are almost severed" (Schwartz, 1974). The group can serve therapeutic (personal), collective, and/or sociopolitical goals. Schwartz's notions of reciprocity and the strength of the group itself as a mutual-aid and self-empowering system are critical in empowerment group work. I refer you to Berman-Rossi's (1994) comprehensive editing of the collected writings of William Schwartz. Papell and Rothman's (1980) conceptualization of the "mainstream model" of social work with groups elaborates on the interactionist approach. These approaches make use of formed or natural groups and can encompass a variety of empowerment purposes. A blending of critical education and conscientization group methods with the interactionist and mainstream models of social work with groups form a foundation for the empowerment group (Lee, 1994). Knowledge of group processes and group-oriented skills "makes it happen." British group-work theorists Mullender and Ward (1991) note that "groups lend themselves to an anti-oppressive style of working" so that process and ends can be one. Their self-directed model also informs the empowerment approach (1991).

COMMUNICATIONS AND WORKERS' ROLES

Goldberg-Wood and Middleman (1989) distinguish types of communication in groups, which may effect the development of the group: "The Maypole," where the worker talks to individuals one-by-one and dominates and controls the group; "The Round Robin," where each participant speaks in turn in relation to a focus given by a worker, and the worker is still in control; "The Hot Seat," where the worker engages in an extended conversation with a member while the others are an audience, and the worker maintains control; "The Agenda Controlled" group, where new and old business and Robert's Rules dominate; and finally "The Free Form," where participants take responsibility to speak with any other person according to the dictates of the moment. Here, the primary responsibility for the flow and form of the work rests with the participants who observe matters of turntaking, consideration, and risking. This latter form of communication is the optimal pattern for empowering groups.

CRITICAL EDUCATION AND CONSCIENTIZATION

The critical education group is the cornerstone of the empowerment group approach from outside of the profession of social work. Paulo Freire developed his critical education approach in Brazil during the 1950s and 1960s: to create a democratically open industrialized society, each citizen needed to develop a critical awareness of realities, and use that awareness to participate in and transform society. Alienated people, particularly poor people, often develop a culture of passive silence and apathy. Freire (1973; 1990; 1994) used critical education to develop literacy and critical thinking.

THE EMPOWERMENT GROUP APPROACH

In summation, the empowerment group utilizes the principles, knowledge base, and skills of the empowerment approach and *explicitly* includes empowerment as purpose, content, process, and outcome of the group's work (Lee, 1991). It includes provision for meeting individual and collective needs through group processes. It can best be described as a mixed goals group form, that is, a blend of individual and shared collective goals where free-form style of communication is used (Goldberg-Wood and Middleman, 1989). To empower, the group must attain its own power. The empowerment group is not a support or mutual-aid group, nor a therapeutic group, nor is it a consciousness-raising or critical-education group, or a political action group. It is all of the above and, by its unique combination of these, more.

GROUP EXAMPLES

To illustrate the empowerment approach in action, I will present excerpts of empowerment group work at My Sisters' Place (MSP), a four-tier program for homeless and formerly homeless women and children in Hartford, Connecticut. These women, the staff, and especially Judith Beaumont (1987), MSP executive director, activist, and my partner in life and in the empowerment group work described here, "coauthored" the empowerment approach.

THE "SUCCESSFUL WOMEN'S GROUP"

Formation

Membership in an empowerment group is a matter of personal choice based on knowledge of the experience. A "try it and see" philosophy helps members who share common ground understand what it is like to be in such a group. In forming an empowerment group for women who had "graduated" from the services of MSP, the co-workers began by inviting large groups of "alumnae" to evening get-togethers. The codes and themes for the empowerment work would emerge from these six meetings, as would a nucleus of women interested in pursuing empowerment together. The format of the evening included a dinner where introductions and an informal style of sharing mutual concerns could take place, and then a formal period of group discussion in which empowerment notions were introduced. Many attended protest activities regarding affordable housing, which coincided with these meetings. Seven African-American women, aged 22 to 34, decided to become the "Alumnae Empowerment Group."

The co-workers started off as more central to the process in helping the group develop a structure and maintain a focus on issues of empowerment, but they soon took on a more advisory role. Within four months, the group developed a club-style structure with a president who called the meetings and maintained the work focus. The group members chose the meeting nights, time, frequency (biweekly), outreach to new members, and the content of the meetings. The workers bolstered the leadership structure, and continued to contribute information and to assist in guiding praxis and reflection on feelings and facts to deepen the work. The group existed for two years, and members still continue to be there for each other. This is an excerpt from a meeting nine months into the life of the group, in which they name themselves:

> Tracey, the President, said "'Alumnae' just don't get it." "Who are we?" asked Vesalie. "We are successful women," said Tracey. "Yeah," said Latoya, "The Successful Women's Group." "No," said Vesalie, "we can't call ourselves that." "Why?" Shandra asked. Vesalie strongly replied, "It implies too much power–that we are powerful." The worker asked if they felt powerful. Vesalie said, "Yes, we are more powerful now; we've got good jobs, we're good mothers, we help others who are homeless, we are meeting our goals, but we haven't gotten there yet." The worker asked, "When you get there, then you have power?" Tracey replied, "But that's just it, we need that power to get there, and we're on our way. Let's convey that we are powerful women, we are successful women. Let's take that name and make it ours. We deserve to walk with that name!" The others strongly agreed. Vesalie thoughtfully accepted this and the name Successful Women was enthusiastically adopted. (Lee, 1994)

Names mean a great deal. The worker's questions here are consciousness-raising questions. This renaming after nine months of meeting represents a 360-degree turn in self-esteem, group pride, and conscientization. The use of codes helped the group achieve this new image.

In the Successful Women's Group, one of the themes that was codified was "barriers to success," The Wall of Barriers. First, the worker asked the group members to define success. It was defined as personal achievement and "people-centered" accomplishments ("giving back to the community").

> The members were asked to imagine and dramatically act out climbing and pulling bricks down from a wall which represented barriers. *The worker posed the critical question: What are the barriers to young African-American women getting over the wall to success for themselves and their people?* Amika was first to try to dramatize it. She said, "The wall is over there; I'm going toward it." "OOPS . . ." she said as she slipped and fell with a great thud, "they greased the ground; I can't even get to the wall. Forget it!" Everyone roared as Amika,

a large, heavily built woman, dramatized falling down in disarray. Tracey said, "It isn't really funny. Amika is right—some of us can't even get to the wall. The grease is prejudice and racism." "And sexism," Ves added, "don't forget that." Shandra said, "Yeah, but determination makes you try and you reach the wall. Like you finish High School and you think you're somewhere, but you didn't take the right courses to go to college so you got to start all over again." Tracey said, "I was angry too when I found out my diploma meant so little . . . ." Shandra unwedged the brick and threw it down hard. Everyone applauded. Ves said, "OK. Watch out! I'm driving this bulldozer right into the wall. The whole thing is coming down. Slam, crash." Everyone cheered her on. "Wait," said Latoya, "a brick hit me; I'm hurt." She wiped imagined blood from her head, "It's the brick of hating myself because I believed 'if you're black, stand back,' and I stood back and didn't go for even what you all went for, a real job and all. But I survived and stand here to tell it. I'm going to get me some too!" Everyone encouraged her. (Lee, 1994)

The use of humor by African Americans and other oppressed groups is an adaptive mechanism. But no one should mistake the seriousness of the meanings in this dramatic enactment and decoding, which was at once both therapeutic and political—leading to a variety of reflections and actions. I now turn to an empowerment group in MSP's program for chronically mentally-ill, formerly homeless women.

Brenda: The Personal/Political Empowerment of a Woman with Mental Illness

Brenda Gary, a 39-year-old African-American woman with multiple physical problems and chronic paranoid schizophrenia, experienced periods of intermittent homelessness for five years. Leaving her children with relatives, she moved cyclically from the streets to the hospital to several shelters. Then she entered MSP's residential support program, which set her up in her own apartment and offered daily support and empowerment services. For the first time since the onset of her illness, Brenda experienced inner peace. Recently Brenda volunteered to testify at public hearings on proposed state

cutbacks of mental health programs. This is an excerpt from a statement (not published) made by Brenda at the hearing:

> We need our programs to keep us aware of life's possibilities.
> No matter what you want to be it's possible. These programs
> kept me on track and looking forward to life. If the State cuts
> these programs, the State also cuts the good that they do . . . We
> have a women's group every week. We talk about what goes on
> in our lives–the problems we experience and solutions to them
> by getting feedback from each other. . .

To get Brenda and her peers to this point, the worker and program director, Gail Bourdon, prepared the empowerment group to
understand the issues and the process of testifying before asking for
their participation. First, Gail shared specific details of the proposed
cuts and elicited the group member's reactions. Gail proposed that
they might want to learn how to testify at the hearings and speak up
for themselves. Then, when interest was high, Gail took two volunteers (Brenda and Vicky) and the staff to a workshop on the legislative process. Two weeks later, during an empowerment meeting,
those who attended the workshop gave a summary of the legislative
process to the group. Brenda volunteered to speak and composed
her testimony that night. The worker recorded the following:

> Early the next evening we went to testify. Brenda patiently
> waited two hours in line and an additional 2 1/2 hours before
> testifying. The testimony was presented in the Hall of the
> House of Representatives. It was a striking image to see
> Brenda, in her woolen hat, speaking so well from the seat of the
> "Minority Leader." (transcribed from agency records)

The group then reflected on their actions in the next meeting. The
worker invited praxis–the members' reflections on the process of
testifying and going to the legislative hearing. Gail records what
follows:

> Group members read the entire *Hartford Courant* article to
> each other. I asked what the women thought and felt about
> attending the hearings. Brenda smiled and proudly stated she

felt good about having spoken. I asked Vicky how she felt about attending the hearing. Vicky said, "It was one of the happiest times in my life. I saw and heard things I never thought I'd even learn about." The entire group cheered . . . I asked Brenda if she thought her message was heard. Brenda said she thought so because they did not ask her unfriendly questions. They accepted her word and even thanked her. I asked the group members who went how it was for them and each replied affirmatively. Vicky added, "I feel like I could do that sometime . . . I feel the strength." The entire group agreed, noting that they had a voice and were heard. Ida said that those who simply sat there also brought support and power in numbers, so they had a presence as well as a voice . . . Brenda added, "It's good to know that I can accomplish things even with a mental illness. Sometimes people think you can't do things because you have a mental illness. I live with the illness, but this does not mean I am not able to take care of business." The other members thoughtfully agreed.

The careful preparation of the members paid off in the group members' confident actions. The skills of guiding praxis helped the members own their gains and expand their understanding and political skills as well as their self-esteem and self-direction. In all of these examples, one can see that personal and political empowerment are part of the same process and outcome.

CONCLUSION

Empowerment practice is gaining in momentum as the oppression of many groups, especially those who are poor, escalates in a reactionary political climate. Like Brenda and the Successful Women, we as social workers face many constraints to operationalizing these concepts. I suggest we construct and deconstruct our own wall of barriers to empowerment practice by joining together to challenge our oppression as professionals and with our groups so we can take care of business too! Then, in the words of Pope John Paul II, speaking in New York City on October 6, 1995, "[In joining together] we will see that the tears of this century have prepared the ground for a new Springtime of the human spirit."

REFERENCES

Addams, Jane (1910). *Twenty Years at Hull House.* Reprinted 1961. New York: Macmillan.

Beaumont, Judith (1987). Prison witness: Exposing the injustice. In Arthur J. Laffin and Anne Montgomery (Eds.), *Swords into Plowshares: Non-Violent Direct Action for Disarmament.* New York: Harper & Row, pp. 80-85.

Berman-Rossi, Toby (Ed.) 1994. *Social Work: The Collected Writings of William Schwartz.* Itasca, IL: Peacock.

Breton, Margot (1992). Liberation theology, group work, and the right of the poor and oppressed to participate in the life of the community. In James A. Garland (Ed.), *Group Work Reaching Out: People, Places, and Power.* Binghamton, NY: The Haworth Press, Inc., pp. 257-270.

Cox, Enid O. (1989). Empowerment of the low income elderly through group work. In Judith A.B. Lee (Ed.), *Group Work with the Poor and Oppressed.* Binghamton, NY: The Haworth Press, Inc., pp. 111-125.

Coyle, Grace (1930). *Social Process in Organized Groups.* Reprinted 1979. Hebron, CN: Practitioners Press.

Estes, Richard (1995). Social development and social work with groups. (Plenary speech presented at the Twelfth Annual Symposium of AASWG, 1991.) In *Proceedings.* Binghamton, NY: The Haworth Press, Inc.

EWAR Project (1992). *A Handbook for Empowering Women in Abusive and Controlling Relationships: Facilitating Critical Thinking in Groups.* Arcata, CA: Humboldt University.

Freire, Paulo (1973). *Pedagogy of the Oppressed.* New York: Seabury.

Freire, Paulo (1990). A critical understanding of social work. *Journal of Progressive Human Services* 1(1):3-9.

Freire, Paulo (1994). *Pedagogy of Hope: Reliving Pedagogy of the Oppressed.* New York: The Continuum Publishing Co.

Germain, Carel B., and Alex Gitterman (1980). *The Life Model of Social Work Practice.* New York: Columbia University Press.

Germain, Carel B., and Alex Gitterman (1996). *The Life Model of Social Work Practice*, 2nd ed. New York: Columbia University Press.

Gitterman, Alex, and Lawrence Shulman (1994). *Mutual Aid Groups, Vulnerable Populations and the Life Cycle.* New York: Columbia University Press.

Goldberg-Wood, Gale, and Ruth R. Middleman (1989). *The Structural Approach to Social Work,* 2nd ed. New York: Columbia University Press.

Gutiérrez, Lorraine (1990). Working with women of color: An empowerment perspective. *Social Work* 35:149-155.

Gutiérrez, Lorraine, and Robert Ortega (1989). Using groups to empower Latinos: A preliminary analysis. In *Proceedings of the Eleventh Symposium.* Akron, OH: AASWG.

Harris, Forrest E., Sr. (1993). *Ministry for Social Crisis: Theology and Praxis in the Black Church Tradition.* Macon, GA: Mercer University Press.

Hartford Courant (March 25, 1995). 1, A9.

Hartford Courant (April 8, 1995). 1, A8.

Hartford Courant (October 1, 1995). Veto of health care bill promised. A3.

Lee, Judith A.B. (1991). Empowerment through mutual aid groups. A practice grounded conceptual framework. *Groupwork* 4(1):5-21.

Lee, Judith A.B. (1994). *The Empowerment Approach to Social Work Practice.* New York: Columbia University Press.

Lewis, Elizabeth (1991). Social change and citizen action: A philosophical explanation for modern social group work. In Abe Vinik and Morris Levin (Eds.), *Social Action in Group Work.* Binghamton, NY: The Haworth Press, Inc., pp. 23-34.

Mancoske, Ronald J., and Jeanne M. Hunzeker (1989). *Empowerment Based Generalist Practice: Direct Services with Individuals.* New York: Cummings and Hathaway.

Mullender, Audrey, and Dave Ward (1991). *Self-Directed Groupwork.* London: Whiting and Birch, Ltd.

Northen, Helen (1994). *Clinical Social Work*, 2nd ed. New York: Columbia University Press.

Papell, Catherine P., and Beulah Rothman (1980). The mainstream model of social work with groups. *Social Work with Groups* 3:5-22.

Parsons, Ruth J. (1989). Empowerment for role alternatives for low-income minority girls: A group work approach. In Judith A.B. Lee (Ed.), *Group Work with the Poor and Oppressed.* Binghamton, NY: The Haworth Press, Inc., pp. 27-46.

Parsons, Ruth J. (1991). Empowerment: Purpose and practice principles in social work. *Social Work with Groups* 14(2):7-21.

Pernell, Ruby B. (1986). Empowerment and social group work. In Marvin Parnes (Ed.), *Innovations in Social Group Work: Feedback from Practice to Theory.* Binghamton, NY: The Haworth Press, Inc., pp. 107-118.

Ryan, William (1971). *Blaming the Victim.* New York: Vintage.

Saleebey, Dennis (Ed.) (1992). *The Strengths Perspective.* New York: Longman.

Schwartz, William (1974). The social worker in the group. In Robert W. Klenk and Robert Ryan (Eds.), *The Practice of Social Work*, 2nd ed. Belmont, CA: Wadsworth, pp. 208-228.

Shapiro, Ben-Zion (1991). Social action, the group, and society. *Social Work with Groups* 14(3/4):7-22.

Shulman, Lawrence (1992). *The Skills of Helping Individuals, Families and Groups.* Itasca, IL: Peacock.

Simon, Barbara Levy (1990). Rethinking empowerment. *Journal of Progressive Human Services* 1(1):29.

Simon, Barbara Levy (1994). *The Empowerment Tradition in American Social Work: A History.* New York: Columbia University Press.

Solomon, Barbara B. (1976). *Black Empowerment: Social Work in Oppressed Communities.* New York: Columbia University Press.

Staub-Bernasconi, Silvia (1991). Social action, empowerment, and social work: An integrating theoretical framework. *Social Work with Groups* 14(3/4):35-52.
West, Cornel (1993). *Race Matters*. Boston, MA: Beacon Press.

Chapter 3

Groups for the Socialization
to Old Age

Margaret E. Betty Hartford
Susan Lawton

Social and psychological needs of well older adults met by group experiences in senior centers and retirement communities can prevent some breakdown from emotional and physical stresses of growing older and may contribute to high-level wellness. Robert Butler, in his classic text, *Aging and Mental Health,* says that for too long we have been concerned with what went wrong rather than considering what can be done in advance to prevent breakdown. "The process of prevention," he says, "requires an understanding of what supports and what interferes with healthy development throughout the course of the life cycle" (Butler and Lewis, 1982). We will examine group experiences specifically offered to prevent breakdown and to encourage wellness for older adults in senior centers and retirement communities.

Many people give little attention to their potential longevity, their futures past age 60, their retirement, or their family patterns. Suddenly they discover that decisions have been made for them. Their jobs disappear or are revamped, even though there is no longer mandatory retirement. Their own health problems or those of their families make unexpected demands on them. New technology resulting in cultural and social changes may alter their lives.

These phenomena may come sooner than expected, as many highly educated and skilled aerospace personnel in our area discovered. It is with shock that these people are confronted with losses of the kinds of satisfaction, identity, schedule, and goals that have been part of their lifestyles all their adult years.

Conversely, some people choose to retire early, wishing to have more time for avocational interests and to travel while they still have the energy. The first few months or even early years of retirement may be happily self-focused, but sooner or later the shock from losses of their previous roles and contacts may set in. They discover that they need to find more meaning, more attachment, more direction in their lives. Butler states that the "major developmental task of aging is to clarify, deepen and find use for what has already been attained in a life time of learning and adapting" (Butler and Lewis, 1982). Thus, people must find places and groups for continuity with their past and make new connections.

Unplanned dramatic changes in living in the later years include losses of spouses, companions, close friends, and associates, leaving individuals in ambiguous states of identity and relationships as well as in grief. Reaching out for new connections and responding to strangers may not come easily for people who always had ready-made associations through work or family. Dealing with grief from these losses may be a new experience in aging.

Other unanticipated changes are physical losses of sight or hearing, or breakdowns in the body (bones, muscles, hearts; respiratory, digestive, or circulatory systems). Changes in physical structure can be a threat to self-image, self-esteem, and integrity, especially in a society that values youth and vigor.

Older people may not run as fast, or at all; they may not see as well to read or drive. They may need more reminders or supports to carry on their tasks of daily living, but generally, older people think of themselves as they have been since young adulthood. A psychic shock challenges the sense of well-being when an older person realizes his or her own aging, when the desire is there to be the same as in young or middle adulthood, but the capacity is different.

So, confronted with inevitable losses and transitions, older people can use the opportunities of group experiences in the retirement community and at the senior center, to be socialized to their life realities, to work through their feelings of loss, and to find meaningful and satisfying roles appropriate for their capacities (Seguin, 1973). As Burnside and Schmidt have written, "If roles in society are given up, then new roles must be found to take their place" (1994). Groups of peers can provide the means of transition to their future.

Butler states, "It is imperative that older people continue to develop and change in a flexible manner if health and mental health are to be promoted and maintained" (Butler and Lewis, 1982).

The tendency for a reactive depression faced by people who have difficulty managing their aging, who feel discontinuity with their productive past, and who lose hope for a satisfying future can be mitigated by supportive group participation. The rich resource of groups in senior centers and retirement communities helps older people come to terms with normal aging and to build new social systems to prevent some of the breakdown resulting from self-devaluation, loss of self-esteem, as well as losses of social relationships and functions in society. They can gratify their needs to stay involved and affirm the importance of their being alive.

The emergence of senior centers has made a shift in potential programs to a wider consumer population beyond bingo, handicrafts, and busy work, encouraging seniors to participate in their own planning and enrichment with adult education, developing new skills, and forming new relationships. Similarly, the emergence of retirement communities, with emphases on self-governance and resident-generated activities programs, has opened opportunities for participation of older adults.

Looking to the future of seniors who will be reaching maturity in the next decade, Gail Sheehy has written that people will be spending more time after their first careers than they did in their work lives. Reaching what has been perceived as old age in their 60s with more vigor, mental capacity, and motivation to be involved, they will experience what she calls second adulthood. They will want additional opportunities to make contributions and to be engaged in satisfying endeavors (Sheehy, 1995). The staff, volunteers, and participants in senior programs who are social workers and gerontologists understand that creating opportunities for participation through group processes serves as a prevention of breakdown and creates an atmosphere of wellness. An administration that is committed to participation through group processes, through team approaches to decision making and leadership, undergirds a preventive program. Furthermore, recognition of the capacities of older people to contribute at a high level, not stereotyped by outmoded concepts of aging, facilitates their wellness.

Newer generations of retirees are demanding opportunities for involvement, though some older people may need to be encouraged to take responsibility for themselves and others, because they have been socialized to disengage and to withdraw from involvement. They may feel it appropriate to act dependent, especially when suffering from losses of roles, relationships, and physical capacities. To create an administrative pattern that uses senior wisdom, experience, and style may take patience and understanding on the part of the administrator in establishing boards and committees, advisory groups, and program planning groups of older people. Philosophically this depends on whether the administration is oriented to goal-directed management, which focuses on production and efficiency, as contrasted to a service-oriented management, which sees process and involvement of older people on their own behalfs as an important part of the goal. The administrator may also need to convince younger community board members and staff that it is appropriate and important to involve seniors as empowered participants on administrative boards and program planning committees.

Older men and women who have managed households, served on boards, worked as teachers, storekeepers, craftspersons, attorneys, executives, and social workers–the gamut of our society–can contribute their talents in many types of administrative groups in senior centers and in retirement communities where they reside. Participation in these groups not only lends strength to the organization at a level of consultation not usually affordable, but reinforces the seniors' strengths and identities. From a prevention standpoint, it gives them a challenge to stay alive and to "be somebody" in their social situations.

People who have had high responsibilities prior to retirement may feel so much loss that given the opportunity to participate, they may try to act as staff themselves, and as single managers, rather than sharing responsibilities with others in group management. The skilled social worker who understands such phenomena will be able to handle these roles and relationships appropriately to maintain a win-win situation. In the end, the program and administration will be strengthened, and the senior participants will attain a higher level of life satisfaction.

SENIOR CENTERS

At the Joslyn Senior Center in Claremont, California, the team approach has been in effect since the creation of the center ten years ago. Current theory in management and administration of both business and social service agencies has rediscovered what group workers have known for decades: that a team-oriented approach that veers away from linear, hierarchical thinking can be as or more productive than the old model, and tends to increase commitment and satisfaction among those involved. In fact, it was through the dynamic effort of a group of Claremont residents of various ages and backgrounds that funds were raised and the senior center constructed.

Inclusive group process has been the standard within the senior program. Groups of staff and volunteers serve administrative, task-oriented functions. Other groups meet for learning, personal enhancement, and support, while others focus on formal and recreational activities.

ADMINISTRATIVE GROUPS

Most notable of these is the involvement of community members in the ongoing development of policies and programs within the Joslyn Senior Center. The Committee on Aging, a standing committee of the city's Human Services Commission, meets monthly to review programs, develop new ideas, and discuss issues of significance to the older adult population. Members of the Committee include retired and still-working business people, college professors and administrators, professionals in services to seniors, and others with an ongoing interest in the well-being of older people.

Some of those providing leadership and service are typical of a growing population that is aging healthier than previous generations, but aging nonetheless. These people, called "young old" by Neugarten (1974), between the ages of 55 and 74, expect the standards of activities and programs at a center they attend to be like other experiences in their lives: sophisticated, meaningful, and reflecting their interests and inputs.

The staff and volunteers of the senior program work with, rather than for, the senior participants. The Committee on Aging regularly meets with other program participants to ask for inputs on the daily lunch program and other services and activities at the center. Ideas are sought from staff and participants in development of program direction.

Many of the scheduled activities at the center are also designed on a participatory group model. A program committee, which oversees the variety of offerings of senior services, includes senior participants as well as professionals from various senior service agencies in the community. Members share ideas from their own experiences and from suggestions others have made to them, and the committee evaluates these ideas in the context of existing programs and perceived needs.

A crisis precipitated the formation of an ad hoc committee with an immediate and serious mission to study and fight a cut in governmental funding to the program. Two years ago, the Los Angeles County Area Agency on Aging withdrew funds for the nutrition program in Claremont, sighting shifting demographics. A group of seniors from the community became active and met with city government and staff to plan a strategy to combat the county's decision. The combined political wisdom and know-how of the committee persuaded the county to modify their policy, and secured essential funding for the nutrition program, which serves hundreds of older adults from the Pomona Valley and is a centerpiece of Claremont's senior program.

EDUCATION, PERSONAL ENHANCEMENT, AND SUPPORT GROUPS

Aside from the obvious bereavement support and the often overlooked substance abuse support groups, there are classes that seek to involve attendees in the process of engagement. Teachers of writing classes organize their formats so that students share their creative expressions with other members of the group and see their responses. A class called "Transitions into Retirement" focuses on the social and psychological aspects of growing older in a safe environment in which people can share anticipated fears and possible satisfactions of life after careers.

ACTIVITY GROUPS

Some groups at the center have a recreational intent, such as the line-dancing class, which brings together older adults with little background in dance, and transforms them into a joyous chorus line. They lose their fears of appearing foolish or clumsy in the nonthreatening, mutually supportive environment of the group, and give themselves up to the satisfaction of movement, sharing, and belonging.

The noon meal program is an example of a less structured group that nonetheless serves to support and strengthen its participants. Volunteers in the kitchen share with paid staff the responsibility of getting the meals to the assembled diners. Those who come to eat often arrive early to meet friends and to share a cup of coffee and a discussion of the day's events before lunch. Activities emerge almost spontaneously from these gatherings, as when people agree to meet at the park on a summer evening to share a potluck supper before a concert. Participants feel a family-like commitment to each other; they check in on friends who fail to come to lunch when expected, and notify the site coordinator of problems when they occur. These lunch program participants may not come to the senior center for any other planned or programmed activity. They may drop in on their lunch breaks from work, or this may be their only outing of the day, but their connections to the center are valuable beyond the obvious provision of nourishment.

The social services/social work aspect of the senior program also reflects a belief in and understanding of the group or team approach. With commitment to an advocacy that stresses empowerment, clients and their families are involved in their own problem solving, and case managers work with other social-work professionals in group care-planning meetings, availing themselves of the benefit of the perspectives and experiences of others to develop more creative approaches in the collaborative process.

Thus, we have an example of a senior center program that recognizes the potential for stress and isolation in aging, and draws seniors into group processes that focus on prevention and wellness.

GROUPS FOR SENIOR PARTICIPATION

Retirement Communities

By the time most people enter a retirement community now, they may have some chronic health problems, have faced some major losses, and have adapted to the initial stresses of retirement. Learning to live in a communal setting, dealing with progressive physical changes, and confronting the end of life are stressful realities for retirement community residents.

Initially people feel some relief from the stresses of living in the wider world, and a security in health provisions, home mainte- nance, food service, and the availability of ready-made neighbors. Couples are reassured that if something happens to one of them the other will be cared for (Dychtwald and Flower, 1989) and those who live alone appreciate the assurance of care when they need it. After relief of becoming a resident and reaction to moving, the flip side of the situation is how people are to feel some responsibility for their own lives. They are challenged to become involved in the activities of the residential community, make new friends and con- nections, and adapt to the institutional structure. They must learn to define themselves in this new setting and make a contribution. The very factors that protect them can lead to their disengagement, and to feelings of anonymity if there are not easy opportunities for becoming connected and for participation. Yet the new generations of aging "will want greater self determination . . . demand resident participation in management decisions and representation on boards," according to a new study by Scruggs (1995).

While older persons may withdraw from the effort of becoming part of the residence, the younger ones may feel frustrated if they cannot take hold immediately and try to manage the place. It is therefore imperative that there be opportunities for all residents to take charge of some part of their lives and those of their neighbors, and for all to find identities within the place and encouragement to participate in the active life of the community to the extent of their capacities.

The yin and yang of retirement community living may confront the professional staff, social workers, and gerontologists, as well as the residents, with challenges to provide resources for prevention of breakdown by assuring involvement through a structure of group experiences.

Administrative Committees

Many retirement communities have small or inactive boards of directors. In the nonprofits, community boards set policy and direct administration. Where such boards exist, there is an opportunity for resident participation with representation of the consumers in policy making and a voice in management. In Mt. San Antonio Gardens, where the author first served on the board and is currently a resident, there are 6 resident members of the community board of approximately 30 members, named by a nominating committee and elected by the corporation. These residents have full board participation in all activities.

In the corporation of this community, administrative committees study issues and make recommendations to the board. The committees, composed of community citizens and including three to five residents, cover issues of admissions, marketing, buildings and grounds, health services, and personnel. An active participatory group process makes it possible for resident members to have a deliberative voice in management, and also a sense of responsibility. This management style of group and team problem solving can happen only when administrative staff recognizes the value of groups in the operation of the organization and encourages group process in their activities. Group participant style has been strongly reinforced at Mt. San Antonio Gardens, sometimes against objections, for the past ten years since a group-work-oriented social worker has been associate director, and retired professionals have served on boards and committees. The structure and process is not by accident.

Not all retirement communities and/or administrators encourage resident involvement. It takes time and patience, and a sense of security on the part of the staff. But for the residents there can be empowerment and participation through group process, especially if channels of communication are kept open. Such a structure provides, as Butler has stated, "optimal growth and adaptation . . . throughout the life cycle when individual strengths and potentials are recognized, reinforced and encouraged by an environment in which he or she lives" (Butler and Lewis, 1982). Currently legislation is pending in California to require all retirement communities to have a written statement on representation of residents on governing boards. The impetus for this legislation came from organized groups of seniors with concerns for the empowerment of all residents of retirement communities to further their senses of control and integrity.

SYSTEM MAINTENANCE GROUPS

Resident Organizations

Some retirement communities have residents councils, which are self-governing bodies for life within the residence. To maintain the highest level of group management, a council is made up of elected representatives of subgroups of residents. With this type of organization, all residents are part of an area that has regularly scheduled meetings to discuss concerns and plan activities appropriate for the area, as well as to hear about other activities in the residence. The council hears reports from each area at monthly meetings. This includes the to-and-from process initially defined by W.I. Newstetter in the social intergroup work process (1948). The council at Mt. San Antonio Gardens is composed of elected officers, members at large, and the area representatives, and is attended by the chair of the board of directors, the president/CEO, and appropriate vice presidents and staff.

That there be open discussion and free group process in the small areas and at the council is crucial to the involvement of residents in roles and functions. Here again the perspective of the group worker gives the group discussion process a high priority, as opposed to legislative structure of parliamentary procedure and formal reporting with hasty convening and dismissal of such groups. It appears that morale, involvement, and personal integrity of residents are better where the emphasis is on individual participation in the group.

Committees' Activities and Functions

Under the auspices of the residents council, many activities are created, organized, and maintained by residents, including as many as 70 committees and functions. This structure gives opportunities for most of the 415 residents to have some roles and responsibilities. The structure prevents isolation and offers alternatives, affirmation, and recognition.

These committees affect the quality of life of all residents. Several committees are integral to the operation of the residence, including food service, resident health services, safety and security, and religious programs. For instance, the food service committee monitors many aspects of this vital component of the residence, and membership on this committee carries with it status appropriate to its importance. It also has an important safety-valve responsibility in the interaction of the residence. Similarly, a residents' health services committee, composed of residents with interests or competencies in health care, oversees health issues for independent residents as well as those in the health center and the assisted care lodge. The committee invites staff participation and maintains a liaison relationship with the Board Health Services Committee, sometimes recommending policy or procedural changes. Since health service is one of the major reasons for living in a retirement community, this vital functioning committee has high status among residents, giving special roles and responsibility to its members.

In all of these groups, residents feed into policy, raise issues and questions, and reduce overdependency and feelings of disenfranchisement, a real preventive and wellness function.

SERVICE PROVISION GROUPS

A large number of groups provide services to the institution and to the residents. Using particular skills of the people, such groups manage the gift shop and the library, and coordinate and produce the lecture series on health, music, education, and current events. A visual aids group provides electronic equipment for people losing their vision. Residents' artwork is exhibited throughout the community by a committee with art and decorating experience.

People who have many of their life tasks taken care of can assume roles and responsibilities in these group tasks that are vital to the organization. Their roles demand excellence in performance, and are in no way superficial activity. Individuals help to make the place run, and improve the quality of life, and they know it.

GROUPS FOR PROVIDING
SOCIAL RELATIONSHIPS

For people for whom it is increasingly difficult to reach out and make new connections, the existence of already formed interest groups provides an easy access. Such social support groups include bridge and other games; the 6:00 a.m. swimmers; the Live Poets, who meet to share their poems with each other; and line dancers. In most of these groups, participation is flexible and fluid. They tend to be low-key, and new members are welcomed. The existence of such groups makes it possible for people to join and be interactive with others whom they might not otherwise meet.

PERSONAL GROWTH GROUPS

Groups of residents who meet to focus on their own growth and enhancement develop spontaneously and change from time to time. The High Level Wellness Group has sponsored workshops on meditation, self-awareness, journal writing, and forums on diet and wellness. In an art workshop, experienced artists and those who would like to learn are helped by a resident teacher. A wood shop is maintained by and very busy with men who like to work with tools.

It has been suggested that there are too many committees at Mt. San Antonio Gardens, and that things could be done more quickly, economically, and efficiently if individuals rather than groups would take the responsibility to run things. Actually, opportunities for resident participation, chances to belong, to make contributions, and to stay connected are crucial to the quality of life of each individual, and make for good group organization. The process usually is more important than the outcome for the well-being of our residents.

CONCLUSION

While the focus of this part of the chapter has been upon the use of group structures within the retirement community to help residents find experiences that will support their growth, integrity, and esteem as they continue to experience the inevitable losses of old age and institutional living, there is no intent to suggest that they become insulated or isolated from the world outside. Residents from the local community are urged to continue their involvement in groups associated with colleges, government, and civic and social activities. Newcomers to the area are given information on volunteer opportunities, and are introduced to community organizations as well as to cultural, political, and environmental groups.

We as social workers, with an understanding of group process and the meaning of groups, and as professionals, staff volunteers, and participants, can contribute our knowledge, skills, and insights wherever we are related to older people. The use of group experiences for the involvement of seniors can prevent breakdown as they confront predictable transitions and threatening changes in their aging lives, and can promote their wellness. We must not let their lives diminish as a result of boredom.

BIBLIOGRAPHY

Burnside, I., and Schmidt, M.G. (1994). *Working with Older Adults, Group Process and Techniques*, Third Edition. Boston: Jones and Bartlett.

Butler, R., and Lewis, M. (1982). *Aging and Mental Health*. St. Louis, MO: C.V. Mosely.

Dychtwald, K., and Flower, J. (1989). *Age Wave, The Challenges and Opportunities of an Aging America*. Los Angeles: Jeremy P. Tarcher.

Hartford, M.E. (1971). *Groups in Social Work*. New York: Columbia University Press.

Hartford, M.E. (1980). The use of group methods for work with the aged. In J. Birren and R.B. Sloan (Eds.), *Handbook of Mental Health and Aging*. Englewood Cliffs, NJ: Prentice Hall.

Neugarten, B. (1974). Age groups in American society and the rise of the young-old. *Ann Am Academy of Political Science*, *415*:187-198.

Newstetter, W.I. (1948). The social intergroup work process. In *Proceedings of the National Conference of Social Work*. New York: Columbia University Press.

Scruggs, D. (1995). *The Future of Continuing Care Retirement Communities*. Washington, DC: American Association of Homes and Services for the Aged.

Seguin, M.M. (1973). Opportunity for peer socialization in a retirement community. *Gerontologist*, *13*:208-214.

Sheehy, G. (1995). *New Passages, Mapping Your Life Across Time*. New York: Random House.

Chapter 4

Psychoeducational Groups: A Model for Recovery and Celebration of the Self

Carol F. Kuechler

DEFINITION AND MODEL IN CONTEXT

The purpose of this chapter is to explore the definition of psychoeducational groups; identify the scope and usefulness of this service form; and present a case example and begin a discussion that bridges the traditions of social work with groups, including client self-determination and empowerment with the principles of andragogy, which guide the educational delivery of emotional, psychological, and behavioral content.

In his description of cognitive treatment in the *Encyclopedia of Social Work*, Granvold (1995) cites the statement that "cognitive" is "probably just as ambiguous as it is popular" (p. 525). Attempting to identify a decisive description or definition could lead one to the same conclusion about "psychoeducational groups." Other attempts to define psychoeducational groups have been made. Kuechler and Andrews (in press) concluded the following about psychoeducational groups:

> . . . [They] are characterized by being time-limited, having a specific group purpose [and] leader-prepared agendas focused on specific content areas, and group structure that facilitates the learning of new information, behaviors and relationship skills. The name comes from their focus on both educating . . . [and] meeting emotional needs.

Focusing on how psychoeducation is distinct from education, Gesme and Kuechler (1995) proposed the following:

> Psycho-education is a process of education where the content focuses on problems related to human development, behavior and relationships e.g., self-esteem, depression, domestic abuse. The psycho-education process invites people *directly* to internalize information for the purpose of behavior change.

They also emphasized that psychoeducation did not include dealing with intrapsychic, psychodynamic aspects of individual motivation or causation, thus distinguishing it from therapy.

When examined in the context of prevention and wellness, psychoeducational groups provide an opportunity to blend the skills of educators and mental health professionals. Burnell and Taylor (1982) reported on a two-year demonstration project that offered a six-week psychoeducational program on stress management as an adjunct to psychotherapy. A case example presented by Gesme and Kuechler (1995) highlighted a class and follow-up support group on self-esteem for adults offered through the health education department of a metropolitan HMO.

Interdisciplinary psychoeducational programs are reported in acute care facilities (Dreier and Lewis, 1991) and schools (Edlefsen and Baird, 1994).

Theoretical Foundations

Kuechler and Andrews (in press) suggested that "Social learning theory and cognitive behavioral perspectives rather than those emphasizing individual psychopathology provide theoretical foundations for psychoeducational groups." Behaviors and skills learned in a familial and societal context can be replaced with new behaviors. Psychoeducational groups provide a "new" learning context "with opportunities to observe and practice new behaviors in a safe, structured setting before trying them out in relationships and interactions outside the group" (Kuechler and Andrews, in press).

This view is congruent with laSalvia's (1993) illustrations of the efficacy of addressing *both* life skills and ego-related issues in outpatient addiction treatment. By including basic information, skill development, and affective issues related to the particular topic/issue being addressed, psychoeducational programs offer opportunities for the synthesis required to achieve new behaviors and support in dealing with the challenges of personal change, whether the focus of the changed behavior is oneself or another family member. Marley (1992) reports on a model incorporating psychoeducation and communication theory to teach families with a mentally ill member empathic awareness and how to manage the member's symptoms and accompanying stress within the family. Psychoeducational programs addressing issues related to chronic illness often include components for the member with the illness and for spouses or other family members with whom they live (e.g., Oshea, Bicknell, and Wheatley, 1991; Iodice and Wodarski, 1987). The knowledge, skills, and support offered by these programs often enable the member to live at home or in the community.

Purpose

The central purpose of these groups is to effect change, usually in the area of behavior. In psychoeducational groups, the focus is on internal application of the material, rather than on learning a series of facts or figures. Psychoeducation is often accompanied by other approaches in a treatment plan, such as medication, therapy, exercise, and other service programs such as day treatment and hospitalization. For example, in a headache treatment program, psychoeducational group sessions included information about headaches, medication management, physical therapy, diet, and stress and pain management skills (Scharff and Marcus, 1994).

Leadership

While leaders of psychoeducational groups vary in their styles, they present information and lead discussion on various issues; teach skills often through the facilitation of role plays; and encourage growth by addressing the affective components of the topic being addressed by the group. Leaders must be knowledgeable in the content area, the dynamics of groups and andragogy (Gesme and Kuechler, 1995; Kuechler and Andrews, in press). For example, in groups for men who batter, skills training may address men getting in touch with their isolation by helping them develop interpersonal support systems.

Leaders are actively involved in the group process. They model behavior as an example for the members and are a central figure in the group in terms of leadership. The structure of a leader-led group offers potency and safety in exploring new behaviors. Group participants value competent leadership to guide their processes of change and growth (Kuechler, 1995).

Leaders guide members to integrate the educational as well as the emotional aspects of the group experience in a structured and non-authoritarian way. This requires skills in leading groups and in teaching adults. Numerous models of group leadership, with a commitment to the empowerment of the members, can be found in the traditions of social group work (e.g., Falck, 1984, 1989, 1993; Gitterman and Shulman, 1986; Glassman and Kates, 1990; Lee, 1994; Pernell, 1986; Simon, 1994).

Knowledge of andragogic teaching methods and processes are important to support the learner as responsible for learning (Knowles, 1970, 1972) and are based on the "ancient insight that the heart of education is learning, not teaching" (Knowles, 1972, p. 33). In this paradigm, leaders become guides and teachers become facilitators. The "leader" of a psychoeducational group must develop skills to inform, guide, and facilitate. Social work group skills may need to be augmented with skills in understanding and responding to a variety of learning styles, and integrating the principles of adult education with those of social work with groups.

FROM "PURE" EDUCATION TO PSYCHOTHERAPY, HOSPITALIZATION, AND MEDICATION

Rather than viewing psychoeducational groups on a continuum, implying a sequence or hierarchy of service delivery, one can view this model in an array or system of services.

Psychoeducational groups for families who had a member with mental illness, including chronic conditions such as schizophrenia (Keefler and Koritar, 1994; Xiong et al., 1994) and depression (Brent et al., 1993; VanGent and Zwart, 1993) were reported.

Programs for people with chemical addiction (laSalvia, 1993; Plasse, 1995) and the impact of culture on treatment (Aguilar et al., 1991) incorporate psychoeducation. Treatment of men who batter and services to the women who have been battered have specific psychoeducational components (Palmer, Brown, and Barrera, 1992).

People and families affected by HIV and AIDS benefited from a variety of psychoeducational groups and programs (Levy et al., 1990; Malow et al., 1994; Pomeroy, 1994; Rhodes, Wolitski, and Thorton-Johnson, 1992; Rounds, Galinsky, and Stevens, 1991).

People in various family forms and life stages are served using psychoeducation: couples (Durana, 1994; Nelsen, 1994); the elderly and those who care for them (Brodaty, Roberts, and Peters, 1994; Huckle, 1994); parents dealing with developmental issues (Cohen and Irwin, 1983; Trad, 1992); and children affected by parental illness (Goldman and Rossland, 1992; Taylor-Brown, Acheson, and Farber, 1993).

Psychoeducational groups and approaches to address mental health issues are reported internationally (Canive et al., 1993; Pereira, 1994; Kaufmann-Ropstad, Karoliussen, and Hoerthe, 1993; Xiong et al., 1994).

Responsible and Effective Practice

Adams (1988) and Lewis (1992) contend that programs that deal with social issues, such as men who batter, must include information and processes that address the societal context. A feminist perspective further defines this societal context as the sociopolitical issues of power and control, male socialization, and the underlying sexist notions that support battering (Adams, 1988).

Psychoeducational groups have been used to develop awareness about behavior and attitudes that may be culturally influenced (Rittner and Nakanishi, 1993) and to train social workers to serve families from an empowering, information-sharing perspective (Gantt et al., 1989). Sensitivity to cultural aspects that may affect treatment have resulted in cultural adaptations to psychoeducational programs (Aguilar et al., 1991).

Toseland and Rivas (1995) report that a series of studies have shown that groups with structure are found to be more effective than groups with less structure. Members appreciate learning strategies to deal with life issues. Yet, support groups have been found to be more effective than a structured group in helping members express their feelings and reach out to others for help (Toseland and Rivas, 1995). Psychoeducational groups provide a model for providing both structure and support when addressing relevant life issues and when led by leaders trained in the content, group process, and teaching of adults.

CASE EXAMPLE: IMPLEMENTATION AND EVALUATION OF THIS MODEL

The implementation and evaluation of a psychoeducational model in a metropolitan HMO with outer-ring satellite offices will be explored. This case focuses on a five-session self-esteem class for adults and an accompanying follow-up educational support group.

Background

The Self-Esteem Support Group was offered to people who had completed introductory and four-week classes. Though there was a fee for the four-week class, the support group was free. The support group typically met for six sessions, every other week. The four-week class was taught by a certified chemical dependency counselor and educator; the support group was cofacilitated by that person and a social worker.

Based on the impetus of informal observations of the leaders and life stories shared by class and group participants, which validated the need and effectiveness of this psychoeducational model, a formal evaluation was conducted. The program evaluation emphasized participant perceptions of self-change and consumer satisfaction.

Study Design

The purpose of this study was to create some exploratory baseline documentation about the nature of the self-esteem class participants, with a particular focus on those who chose to participate in the follow-up support group. The information would help determine the usefulness of the support group in order to make decisions about continuing formats, such as offering the support group in other locations and instituting a fee.

In July 1995, current and former support group participants were invited by the cofacilitators, through the auspices of the HMO, to participate in a focus group. Letters were sent to approximately 75 people. Because of the voluntary nature of participation and no-cost basis, there is no institutionalized method for tracking people who participate in the support group. This limits the information available for comparison of respondents to the overall population of self-esteem class participants.

Study Results

Introduction to Self-Esteem and Self-Esteem for Adults

During the class sessions of 1995, descriptive data were collected from participants of the introductory and four-week self-esteem classes on a voluntary basis. Members were asked to report gender, age, referral source, other resources used (classes, therapy), and medication. Results of gender, age, and medication were difficult to track due to the voluntary nature of the information request. Participants in the four-week class were also invited to complete the Coopersmith Self-Esteem Inventory at the beginning and end of the class and asked to use a form of identification to match results on an anonymous basis. Not all class members completed pre/postinventories; some did not include age and gender information, and some did not use any, or consistent, identifiers. The results of gender, age, and pre- and post-Coopersmith scores were inadequate for data analysis. Since the total number of participants for each cohort was not available, it was not possible to assess how representative the completed information was for either the introductory or four-week classes.

Self-Esteem Support Group

Four people attended the focus group and one person responded in writing to the questions that had been sent with the invitation letter and meeting time. These findings must be considered exploratory, though many do concur with anecdotal reports by members to the group leader.

Participants were asked to discuss their motivations for deciding to join the support group, their goals, skills learned, and what was most and least helpful. They were asked about the length of time they participated and for recommendations about what to continue and what to change. Respondents stated that they had gotten so much from the support group they wanted to give something back and to do what they could to have the support group continue. In addition to unanimous praise for the caring competence of the course facilitator, respondents agreed with one woman who articulated the importance of having a qualified leader for the support group as well as for the class. Her response included a statement of trust in her health care provider to choose qualified leaders, who are able to guide and instruct. They clearly viewed the support group sponsored by their HMO as distinct from other resources in the community.

Virtually the only frustration expressed had to do with the process of communicating the support group schedule on a regular basis to all people who were qualified to participate. This is likely to be a reflection of the informal status of the support group in the organization. Since no fees are collected, the educational support group is not advertised nor is attendance monitored in any way. This open structure was also cited as positive by the respondents, having the support group available regardless of how many people might show up on any one night, or during any six-week session.

Major Findings

The support group offers participants an opportunity to integrate the information and skills introduced during the four-week class into their daily lives. In particular, participants valued the opportunity to

- practice new skills and attitudes in a safe environment;
- learn from others who have similar strengths, concerns, and needs;
- have guidance and input from a qualified leader while they learn;
- come and go in support group sessions based on personal need; and
- have the support group available on a no-cost basis.

Communication about when and where support group sessions will be held is critical to facilitating participation. Participants addressed the following issues:

- Knowing the schedule to facilitate continuation and rejoining
- Directions to/through the new facility
- Offering the support group in other locations

Recommendations Offered to the HMO

- Continue offering the educational support group as a follow-up to the self-esteem class.
- Offer a leader-facilitated support group at no cost to participants.
- Establish a standard schedule of support group sessions.
- Develop and support a mailing list of self-esteem class participants and send notices of the support group schedule on a regular basis.
- Remind people of the opportunity to retake the basic four-week class.

HMO Program Response to Study Findings and Recommendations

Within weeks of the study's completion, and prior to the fall session of support groups, the Health Education Coordinator had accomplished the following:

- Developed a brochure to all past class attendees with the session schedule, a map to the facility, and an invitation to retake the four-week class if they wanted to
- Established a standard six-week schedule and a complete mailing list of past self-esteem class participants
- Initiated a nominal fee for the support group, including a coupon system with several free sessions as a transition for newcomers (K. Van Guilder, personal correspondence, September 6, 1995)

Summary

The scope of this case example is narrow compared to the range of literature, which includes many examples of the use of psychoeducational groups. It does, however, highlight the importance of integrating psychoeducation into the systems and structures of care and healing. It is an effective service delivery method responsive to the increasing concerns of cost effectiveness, emphasis on "brief therapy," waiting lists for therapy/service, and client satisfaction. Social workers skilled in the development and conduct of these groups have unique opportunities to respond to the growing pressures from agencies and clients to provide relevant, responsive, and time-oriented services.

Providing opportunities for psychoeducational groups increases the likelihood of addressing "prevention" needs before they develop into crisis needs. Likewise, as has been demonstrated in a variety of studies, "maintenance" in services to people with chronic physical and mental illnesses serves the same function as prevention, enabling people to live at home and in the community rather than be hospitalized. When psychoeducation programs are initiated, they should meet the standards of responsible program development by stating specific learning and behavioral goals, and measuring in a variety of ways how they have been met.

FOCUS GROUP QUESTIONS

1. What led to your decision to join the support group?

   How long after the class did you join?
   How long did you stay in the group?

2. What were your goals in joining the support group?

   If you started with no specific goals, did you develop some as you were in the group?
   Did your goals change over time?
   If so, how?

3. What skill(s) did you learn?

   How were they helpful?
   Which ones are you still using?

4. What was most helpful about participating in the support group?

   What was least helpful?

5. What would you recommend keeping?
6. What changes would you recommend?
7. Is there anything else you would like to add?

REFERENCES

Adams, D. (1988). Treatment models of men who batter: A profeminist analysis. In *Feminist Perspectives on Wife Abuse*, K. Yllo and M. Bograd (Eds.). Newbury Park, CA: Sage Publications, pp. 176-199.

Aguilar, M.A., DiNitto, D.M., Franklin, C., and Lopez-Pilkinton, B. (1991). Mexican-American families: A psychoeducational approach for addressing chemical dependency and codependency. *Child and Adolescent Social Work*, 8(4):309-326.

Brent, D.A., Poling, K., McKain, B., and Baugher, M. (1993). A psychoeducational program for families of affectively ill children and adolescents. *Journal of the American Academy of Child and Adolescent Psychiatry*, 32(4):770-774.

Brodaty, H., Roberts, K., and Peters, K. (1994). Quasi-experimental evaluation of an educational model for dementia caregivers. *International Journal of Geriatric Psychiatry*, 9(3):195-204.

Burnell, G.M. and Taylor, P.H. (1982). Psychoeducational programs for problems in living. *Health and Social Work*, 7(1):7-13.

Canive, J.M., Sanz-Fuentenebro, J., Tuason, V.B., Vazquez, C., Schrader, R.M., Alberdi, S., and Fuentenebro, F. (1993). Psychoeducation in Spain. *Hospital and Community Psychiatry*, 44(7):679-681.

Cohen, M. and Irwin, C.E. (1983). Parent-time: Psychoeducational groups for parents of adolescents. *Health and Social Work*, 8(3):196-202.

Dreier, M.P. and Lewis, M.G. (1991). Support and psychoeducation for parents of hospitalized mentally ill children. *Health and Social Work*, 16(1):11-18.

Durana, C. (1994). The use of bonding and emotional expressiveness in the PAIRS training: A psychoeducational approach for couples. *Journal of Family Psychotherapy*, 5(2):65-81.

Edlefsen, M., and Baird, M. (1994). Making it work: Preventive mental health care for disadvantaged preschoolers. *Social Work*, 39(5):566-573.

Falck, H. (1984). The membership model of social work. *Social Work*, 29(2):155-160.

Falck, H. (1989). The management of membership: Social group work contributions. *Social Work with Groups*, 12(3):19-32.

Falck, H. (1993). Central characteristics of social work with groups: A socio-cultural analysis. Invitational paper presented at the 15th annual meeting, Association for the Advancement of Social Work with Groups, New York City.

Gantt, A., Hopkins, M., Pinsky, S., and Tuzman, L. (1989). The training of social work students in the psychoeducation model of family treatment. *Journal of Teaching in Social Work*, 3(1):35-43.

Gesme, C.A. and Kuechler, C.F. (1995). New fruit for the wine: Using psychoeducational groups. The origins and continuing development of transactional analysis: First major international TA conference. (International Transactional Analysis Association, 33rd Annual Conference, San Francisco, CA; August.) Transcript.

Gitterman, A. and Shulman, L. (1986). *Mutual aid groups and the life cycle.* Itasca, IL: F.E. Peacock Publishers, Inc.

Glassman, U., and Kates, L. (1990). *Group work: A humanistic approach.* Newbury Park, CA: Sage Publications.

Goldman, B.M. and Rossland, S. (1992). Young children of alcoholics: a group treatment model. *Social Work in Health Care, 16*(3):53-65.

Granvold, D.K. (1995). Cognitive treatment. In *Encyclopedia of social work,* 19th Edition. Washington, DC: NASW Press, pp. 525-538.

Huckle, P.L. (1994). Families and dementia. *International Journal of Geriatric Psychiatry, 9*(9):735-741.

Iodice, J.D. and Wodarski, J.S. (1987). Aftercare treatment for schizophrenics living at home. *Social Work, 32*(2):122-128.

Kaufmann-Ropstad, I., Karoliussen, L., and Hoerthe, K. (1993). A psychoeducational and cognitive treatment program for adolescents with schizophrenia: Results after 2 years. *Annales Medico Psychologiques, 151*(4):336-339.

Keefler, J. and Koritar, E. (1994). Essential elements of a family psychoeducation program in the aftercare of schizophrenia. *Journal of Marital and Family Therapy, 20*(4):369-380.

Knowles, M. S. (1970). *The modern practice of adult education: From andragogy versus pedagogy.* Chicago: Association Press/Follett.

Knowles, M.S. (1972). Innovations in teaching styles and approaches based upon adult learning. *Education for Social Work,* (Spring):32-39.

Kuechler, C.F. (1995, August). Report on focus group evaluation of self-esteem for adults support group. Prepared for Park Nicollet Health Education Department. St. Louis Park, MN.

Kuechler, C.F. and Andrews, J. (1996). Providing a bridge between psychoeducational groups and social work. *Transactional Analysis Journal., 26*(2):175-181.

laSalvia, T.A. (1993). Enhancing addiction treatment through psychoeducational groups. *Journal of Substance Abuse Treatment, 10*(5):439-444.

Lee, J.B. (1994). *The empowerment approach to social work practice.* New York: Columbia University Press.

Levy, R.S., Tendler, C., VanDevanter, N., and Cleary, P.D. (1990). A group intervention model for individuals testing positive for HIV antibody. *American Journal of Orthopsychiatry, 60*(3):452-459.

Lewis, E. (1992). Regaining promise: Feminist perspectives for social group work practice. *Social Work with Groups, 15*(2/3):271-284.

Malow, R.M., West, J.A., Corrigan, S.A., Pena, J.M., and Cunningham, S.C. (1994). Outcome of psychoeducation from HIV risk reduction. *AIDS Education and Prevention, 6*(2):113-125.

Marley, J.A. (1992). Content and context: Working with mentally ill people in family therapy. *Social Work, 37*(5):412-417.

Nelsen, J.C. (1994). One partner impaired: Implications for couple treatment. *Family Therapy, 21*(3):185-196.

Oshea, M.D., Bicknell, L., and Wheatley, D. (1991). Brief multifamily psycho-education programs for schizophrenia: Strategies for implementation and management. *The American Journal of Family Therapy, 19*(1):33-44.

Palmer, S.E., Brown, R.A., and Barrera, M.E. (1992). Groups treatment program for abusive husbands: Long term evaluation. *American Journal of Orthopsychiatry, 62*(2):276-283.

Pereira, M.J. (1994). Aplicación de la terapía familiar y del modelo psicoeducativo en una unidad de internamiento breve/Family therapy and psychoeducation in a short-term hospitalization unit. *Psiquis Revista de Psiquiatría, Psicológia y Psicosomática, 15*(1):43-47.

Pernell, R.B. (1986). Empowerment and social group work. In *Innovations in social groupwork*. In M. Parnes (Ed.), *Feedback from practice to theory*. Binghamton, NY: The Haworth Press, Inc., pp. 107-117.

Plasse, B.R. (1995). Parenting groups for recovering addicts in a day treatment center. *Social Work, 40*(1):65-74.

Pomeroy, E.C. (1994). A psychoeducational group intervention for family members of persons with AIDS: An effectiveness study. (Doctoral dissertation, University of Texas at Austin.) *PsycLIT, 30*(3), No. 877.

Rhodes, F., Wolitski, R.J., and Thorton-Johnson, S. (1992). An experiential program to reduce AIDS risk among female sex partners of injection-drugs users. *Health and Social Work, 17*(4):261-272.

Rittner, B. and Nakanishi, M. (1993). Challenging stereotypes and cultural biases through small group process. *Social Work with Groups, 16*(4):5-23.

Rounds, K.A., Galinsky, M.J., and Stevens, L.S. (1991). Linking people with AIDS in rural communities: The telephone group. *Social Work, 36*(1):13-18.

Scharff, L. and Marcus, D.A. (1994). Interdisciplinary outpatient group treatment of intractable headache. *Headache, 34*(2):73-78.

Simon, B.L. (1994). *The empowerment tradition in American social work: A history.* New York: Columbia University Press.

Taylor-Brown, J., Acheson, A., and Farber, J.M. (1993). Kids can cope: A group intervention for children whose parents have cancer. *Journal of Psychosocial Oncology, 11*(1):41-53.

Toseland, R.W. and Rivas, R.F. (1995). *An introduction to group work practice.* New York: Macmillan Publishing Company.

Trad, P.V. (1992). The application of previewing: Preventive caregiver-infant psychoeducational groups. *Journal of Child and Adolescent Group Therapy, 2*(1):31-51.

VanGent, E.M. and Zwart, F.M. (1993). Ultra-short versus group therapy in addition to lithium. *Patient Education and Counseling, 21*(3):135-141.

Van Guilder, K. (1995). Personal correspondence, September 6.

Xiong, W., Phillips, M.R., Xiang, H., Dai, Q., Kleinman, J., Kleinman, A., and Wang, R. (1994). Family-based intervention for schizophrenic patients in China: A randomised controlled trial. *British Journal of Psychiatry, 165*(2):239-247.

Chapter 5

Conflict Management in Group Treatment: "Get Out of My Face, You S.O.B.!"

Kenneth E. Reid

Conflict in groups is inevitable. How the conflict is managed–or mismanaged–will have impact on both individual and group dynamics. Unmanaged conflict leads to chaos while submerged conflict results in apathy or passive aggressive behavior. Virtually all clients enter treatment because of some form of conflict in their lives. It may be expressed internally, through interpersonal relationships, or externally through struggles with social, legal, familial, or other external systems. As participants in the group share the same space and the same leader at the same time, they will experience conflict with each other as well as with the leader.

While much has been written about the role of the worker in group treatment, the recognition and management of conflict in groups has received limited attention. It is imperative for the worker to know how to handle friction and strife in the group in order to assist clients in developing self-confidence and communication skills. The goal of this chapter is to provide a conceptual base for understanding conflict and group members' behaviors when in conflict, and to offer recommendations for managing and making therapeutic use of conflict on behalf of the clients.

DEFINING CONFLICT

Conflict, by definition, is a sharp disagreement or collision in interests and ideas. Derived from the Latin *conflictus*–a striking

61

together with force–it denotes opposition, discord, and friction. For many, the word conflict connotes something stronger such as battle, aggression, destruction, and rage. It evokes feelings of anguish and pain, and is viewed as something to be avoided or settled as rapidly as possible.

According to the literature, conflict in groups results when two or more people perceive that their individual goals are mutually exclusive; that is, accomplishing one person's goal keeps another's goal from being achieved (Lumsden and Lumsden, 1993). Hocker and Wilmot (1991) view conflict as an expressed struggle between at least two interdependent parties who perceive incompatible goals, scarce resources, and interference from the other party in achieving their goals. Inherent in this definition is the notion that conflict involves *expressed* communication. Whereas a person may experience internal distress, it becomes conflict when it is actually expressed. The word *perceive* is also significant in that nothing automatically labels a situation as conflictual; instead, conflict depends on how people define a particular situation.

Conflict in the small treatment group is both unavoidable and necessary. It is unavoidable in that clients bring to the group their past struggles, and repeat these struggles within the group. It naturally emerges as part of the worker-member involvement in the form of potential disagreement between the worker and the members, member and member, and the group and other groups. Conflict is a necessary part of the treatment process as it provides the individuals a means to gain insights, practice new behaviors, stimulate more successful communications, and produce helpful changes in client attitudes. Conflict in the small group may involve the group's task, which is content, and how things are done, which is process.

WORKER AMBIVALENCE

While clients may be uncomfortable with conflict, workers are, at best, ambivalent about conflict. We pay lip service to the conventional wisdom that conflict is essential in the growth and development of the individuals and the group. Practitioners and social scientists, however, tend to accentuate the negative effects of conflict, putting inordinate energy into explaining the causes and figuring out means for its resolution. Worchel, Coutant-Sassic, and Wong (1993) report that in their examination of the interpersonal relations, group dynamics, and intergroup relations literature, conflict was presented as a "villain, a destroyer of relationships, and something to be exorcised as soon as possible lest it taint the interaction."

When conflict occurs in the group, workers often become anxious and unwittingly go about suppressing it or bringing about its early reconciliation. To keep control, there may be the temptation to accentuate less troublesome therapeutic values such as empathy, acceptance, and kindly understanding as a means of promoting member self-esteem and communications skills. We may fear that members' feelings will be hurt and that those involved will emotionally withdraw or not return to the group. Or, even worse, we fear that the group will disintegrate and breakup.

Unseasoned workers, in particular, fear that they will be judged inadequate from the stormy interaction, and the group perceived as out of control. They may fear that members won't like them and denounce them to other clients. As a response, the worker assumes the role of mediator, savior, or "Red Crosser," defending the confrontee, chiding the confronter and, in general, pouring oil on the waters of conflict (Egan, 1970).

Of course, any or all of the above may occur. Members do get angry and yell. Feelings get hurt and individuals withdraw or don't return to the group. Furthermore, workers may find themselves explaining, with some chagrin, to a supervisor the reason for the members' passionate expressions of feelings, loud voices, and why a participant slammed the door as that person prematurely exited the session. Furthermore, there are clients who the worker will never please no matter how hard he or she tries.

POSITIVE EFFECTS OF CONFLICT

It is safe to say that conflict plays a role at all levels of human interaction, whether intrapersonal, interpersonal, or intergroup. It is also a significant element in the course of a group's development. Yalom (1995) observes that the absence of conflict, in fact, suggests some impairment of the group's developmental sequence. Members can, in a variety of ways, profit from conflict provided that appropriate group norms have been established, and intensity of the conflict does not exceed the members' tolerance. There needs to be a balance between too much and too little conflict in the group in that either extreme hinders cohesion and growth.

Individuals grow as they struggle to make reasonable and realistic decisions in their lives. Conflict arising within individuals making decisions forces them to examine their self-concepts and to consider the issues involved in the decisions. Festinger (1957) writes that such conflicts, particularly in group situations, motivate individuals to guard their self-concepts by seeking evidence to support their decisions. While their search process is far from objective, such conflict has the potential of creating a better-informed individual who has considered the positive as well as the negative aspect of a chosen course of action. Conflict too, has the potential of surfacing problems and forcing them to be dealt with. It can stimulate and energize individuals, motivate the search for creative alternatives, and provide vivid feedback.

When disputes occur openly within a group, conflict can expose important misconceptions and clarify distorted perceptions members have of one another. Disagreements can increase the level of self-disclosure within a group as members reveal more of themselves in an effort to back up their points. For individuals who are passive and uninvolved, conflict can increase a sense of assertiveness. Timid people, when involved in a struggle with another member, can learn what it feels like to hold firm and be victorious rather than giving in to the will of another at the first sign of resistance. Overly aggressive people, for whom losing represents the threat of humiliation, can learn how beneficial, even rewarding, it can be to admit defeat and modify oneself in response to a "worthy opponent's" demands (Nicholas, 1984).

Individuals can learn that anger does not necessarily result in rejection. Danesh (1977) writes that because aggression, hostility, and violence are normally considered unacceptable, people are reluctant to show or acknowledge anger. When failure to control anger brings disapproval from others, it creates anxiety and guilt in the angry person. Anger becomes equated with hate and considered to be the opposite of love. As a result, the person who is unable to control his or her angry thoughts, feelings, or actions becomes fearful that the anger will be interpreted as a sign of lack of sincerity and love, and he or she grows anxious out of a fear of rejection.

PERSONAL CONFLICT-RESPONSE MODES

In the beginning stages of a group, we become aware of the characteristics of the various members. Some, we discover, are kind, gentle, and friendly, while others appear rude, obnoxious, and overbearing. Some clearly are there to work, while others are self-absorbed and unwilling to look at their own actions. Some may try to dominate the group, and others are withdrawn, aloof, and distant. Some members take the group very seriously and are concerned with the outcome, while others do not want to be there and have little concern with the outcome. Some members are very sensitive to the feelings of other members, while still others are unaware how they impact their fellow members.

The member's interpersonal style in the group will be similar to his or her interactional style outside the group. If, for example, the person is hostile and overbearing outside the group, these same behaviors will be exhibited in the group. Similarly, if the person is passive in relationships with friends and fellow workers, passive behaviors will be visible as he or she relates to other members.

The member's cultural background can also be a determinant as to how he or she experiences and responds to conflict in the group. The western orientation to treatment is based on an individualistic value perspective that rewards directness, openness, and assertiveness. Other cultures view these same attributes as discourteous and something to be avoided. Various Latin-American cultures, for example, value finding indirect ways of asking for what you want rather than asking for it directly (Atkinson, 1995). Asian-American and other cultures use indirect communication to avoid causing shame or loss of face to others and to maintain harmonious relations (Chu and Sue, 1984; Leong, 1992). These cultures view it as impolite to challenge authority, interrupt others, appear verbally assertive, and voice negative comments in public.

Gender differences influence the extent to which groups are cooperative or competitive. Males and females in groups tend to follow conventional sex roles, with women characteristically listening and seeking agreement, and males interrupting and advising (Tannen, 1990). Bond and Vinacke (1961), studying coalition formation, observed that males and females differed in their basic strategies toward working with others. Males engaged the group task in a competitive fashion with a strong motivation toward winning, whereas females appeared to be more concerned with social and ethical considerations. Furthermore, male leaders who lead groups containing both male and female members tend to be challenged more by male members than those leaders in all-male groups (Eskilson and Wiley, 1976).

Another key determinant of behavior is the individual's primary orientation in dealing with conflict. Each group participant–as well as the worker–responds to conflict differently. Thomas and Kilmann (1974), considering conflict from an organizational vantage point, categorize five dominant orientations or modes of dealing with conflict–competing, accommodating, collaborating, sharing, and avoiding:

1. *Competing* is an orientation or response that involves an emphasis on winning one's own concerns at the expense of another's. This is a power-oriented mode with efforts to force and dominate the other, typically in a "win-lose" fashion.
2. *Accommodating* is both unassertive and cooperative, concentrating on appeasement and trying to satisfy the other participants without attention to one's own concerns. There is a flavor of self-sacrifice in this mode, with selfless generosity, giving in to the other, and acquiescing.
3. *Collaborating* is a mode that places emphasis on satisfying the concerns of all parties and working with others in a collaborative fashion to find an alternative that integrates and fully satisfies the concerns of all. This mode is both assertive and cooperative and requires a relatively large investment in time and energy to accomplish such joint problem solving.
4. *Sharing* is an orientation that suggests bargaining and compromise and reflects a preference for partial satisfaction of the concerns of both parties. It might mean trading concessions, splitting the difference, or finding a middle ground.

5. *Avoiding* is a mode that reflects inattention to the others involved. It is neither assertive nor cooperative.

Each of these five modes have value, and no single mode is always good or always bad in all situations. Each participant will tend to be more comfortable with certain types of behaviors in conflict situations. Similarly, most individuals tend to make predominant use of one or several of the modes, while making relatively less use of the others.

There are clients whose responses to conflict are so excessive that they present real challenges for the group and its leader. Because of their character structures, they will invariably be involved in conflicts and will engender conflicts in any group to which they belong (Yalom, 1995). Examples of these clients are those individuals who avoid conflict at all costs, assuming that it is a sign of something intrinsically wrong, and then over-react when it occurs; or those clients who thrive on conflict and even enjoy it as they satisfy a drive for identity, power, or a sense of adequacy; or those who are not adept at any other mode of behavior, and overuse conflict without any obvious constructive outcome.

Individuals such as those suffering from paranoid ideation may be externally sensitive to hostilities that are latent in the group. They may be compelled to ferret out and ignite these tensions, usually becoming embroiled in struggles from which they find it difficult to withdraw. When a group is not cohesive, and/or when the paranoid person is feeling particularly mistrustful, he or she can, according to Nicholas (1984), tear the group apart with conflict.

Conflict is usually first expressed in the form of a complaint. The complaint might be internally generated, as is the case with someone who is experiencing physical symptoms, depression, or difficulty with a relationship. Or it can be externally generated, as is characteristic of many court-referred or substance abuse clients. In most instances, the complaint will not be isolated but part of a pattern of behavior or symptomatology that arises repeatedly in the client's life. These symptoms and behaviors tend to resurface in the group, and the conflicts that initially brought the client into treatment eventually manifest as conflicts with the worker and group members (Unger, 1990).

SOURCES OF GROUP CONFLICT

The actual sources of disagreement in a group are many. Most common is the natural difference in outlook based on the members' life experiences and perceptions. Usually after further exploration of the problem or situation, it becomes clear that there is a misunderstanding and no real conflict exists. In other instances the disagreements are real and have relevance to the group, but can be easily solved by changing some minor situational factor, for example: a group member who wants to smoke during the sessions but is reminded of the agency's no-smoking policy; the member who is constantly late for sessions, and told by the worker he will have to arrive on time or drop out of the group; or several members who disagree over whether or not to move to another room, and who are silenced when a vote is taken. Such disagreements are generally easily solvable without any undue increase in group tension.

Frank (1955) and Yalom (1995) note that in the early stages of the group there is often antagonism between members largely based on the contempt that members have for each other. Such contempt, usually a projection of a member's self-contempt, may go on for several months before the person begins to hear and respect the opinions of other members. There may also be rivalry for the leader's attention with various individuals vying for the position of most-favored-member status.

There may be transference in which a member responds to other members or the worker, not on the basis of reality but on the basis of an image of the other, distorted by past relationships as well as current interpersonal needs and fears. Mirroring–or mirror reaction–results when a member's unconscious hostility is triggered when he or she encounters another person who embodies these very traits. The response may be shunning the person or experiencing a strong but inexplicable antagonism toward him or her.

While the potential for conflict is present during every stage of a group's life, most theories of group development identify a particular stage when conflict is more salient. Typically, group conflict first appears after an initial period wherein members "feel each other out" and present their most attractive selves. This is also a period in which members evaluate the worker's ability to create a safe environment for the expression of antagonistic or conflict-provoking feelings (Unger, 1990).

Whether or not conflict surfaces will largely depend on the group members' perceptions of the worker as someone who can tolerate and manage the inevitable conflicts that will develop as the members become mutually involved.

Tuckman (1965) refers to this second stage as a period of storming and norming because the members become hostile toward one another and toward the worker as a means of expressing their individuality and resisting the formation of group structure. Sarri and Galinsky (1967) refer to it as the revision phase because there is a challenge to the existing group structure accompanied by a modification of the group's purposes and operating procedures. Reid (1991), using a life-span metaphor, likens the stage to that of adolescence because of the struggle for identity, power, and differentiation.

ANGER TOWARD THE LEADER

The occurrence of anger toward the group leader is unavoidable. Part of this is a result of the member's unrealistic expectations as to the worker's potential therapeutic power, and how the change process will occur. Sometimes the members' hopes are so grand that regardless of the social worker's competence, there will be disappointment. The process of disenchantment occurs as members recognize the worker's personal and professional limitations. An example of this is the member's mistaken belief that the worker has the ability to know all and to heal all. When it becomes obvious that the worker does not have the answers and, in fact, it is up to the members to find their own answers, there is a sense of betrayal (Reid, 1991).

Seldom is the attack on the worker unified. As some members challenge the worker, others defend the worker. Once the attack is over, often there is increased independence among the members. Hansen, Warner, and Smith (1980) write that the worker may feel that he or she no longer plays such a necessary part in the group and that his or her roles are being partially filled by the members. The worker may be viewed more realistically with other members in the group offering interpretations, and confronting and adopting the leader's techniques. While a worshipful attitude is still present, it is detached from the personhood of the worker. Seldom will another group member be invested with the leader's attributes as this will be met with sibling rivalry.

Ironically, the process of members challenging the worker frequently results in a deeper commitment by the member to the group process and a higher investment in the group's future (MacKenzie, 1990). Not surprisingly, this process often has an adolescent quality to it. It is as if the members know that some of the issues they are raising are of less than central importance, yet they are bound to vigorously make their points. MacKenzie (1990) notes that just as teenagers establish close peer relationships, group members band together as "co-rebels" determined to alter the system.

CONFLICT MANAGEMENT STRATEGIES

While it would be natural to think in terms of conflict resolution, a more apt term is conflict management. Resolution is an absolute that suggests a static state. Because much of the conflict dealt with in the group is a result of interpersonal style, resolution of conflict–once and for all–is seldom possible nor is it desirable in a group treatment situation. Even though a single issue is resolved, the sources of conflict remain and the potential for conflict continues. Consequently, our therapeutic objective becomes that of creating a group environment that allows conflicts to arise and to be explored, and turned into positive growth experiences for the members. This is never easy, especially when the worker feels under pressure to do something (Reid, 1991).

Establishing Norms

Early in the group, it is important for the worker to develop norms for dealing with anger, confrontation, and conflict, as well as safety. These norms typically include acceptance and encouragement of conflict, as long as the issues are addressed openly and honestly. As the group progresses, it can both model and communicate conceptually about such norms, affirming the importance of openness by group members–especially in conflictual situations.

Clients sometimes enter groups with the idea that they are free to behave and express themselves exactly as they wish. Such individuals may become resentful when presented with norms of conduct for the group. Expectations of what is acceptable and what is not need to be made clear. If members have histories of physical aggression, the norm of "no violence" needs to be underscored; that is, members may not engage in violence or threats of violence.

Deviation from the group's norms can be expected. Exactly how the members deviate from or resist the norms often tells a great deal about the way they deal with conflict in their everyday lives. Clients tend to resent these limitations placed on their behaviors, but particularly in the early stage of the group, are unwilling to confront the worker directly with their resentments. The tendency is for the clients to either bicker with each other or to band together—usually unconsciously—and to be uncooperative (Unger, 1990).

Dealing in the Here-and-Now

The small group provides a rich interpersonal context wherein individuals' overlearned, habitual, and reactive patterns become evident. There will be a tendency to structure their experiences within the group in dysfunctional but familiar ways. This occurs as group members try to elicit behaviors and reactions from the worker and group members that conform to and confirm their perceptions.

Strachey (1934), commenting on dealing with the present versus the past, writes the following:

> Instead of having to deal as best we may with conflicts of the remote past, which are concerned with dead circumstances and mummified personalities and whose outcome is already determined, we find ourselves in an actual and immediate situation in which we and the patient are the principal characters.

Working in the here-and-now involves addressing immediate feelings and interactions within the group. An illustration is the group member who, without awareness, frequently offended his friends and family because of his apparent lack of interest in what they said. Instead of listening, he was one step ahead, thinking and planning what he was going to say next. This very same behavior manifested itself in the group with fellow members complaining that he never seemed to listen, and that he was responsible for misunderstandings and for their need to repeat themselves. The worker conveyed her own sense of being "tuned out" when she made observations and interpretations to him. Awareness of the pattern, fostered by feedback from the members and the worker, brought the issue to the surface and provided a laboratory to work on his self-defeating patterns.

Generally, focusing on relational issues should wait until rapport and trust have developed. This is crucial in helping the client endure the vulnerability, threat, and psychological pain at times associated with personal encounter from the other members.

Keeping Calm

One of the most important things workers need to do when conflict surfaces is to remain calm. This communicates to the members the commanding message that in spite of what is occurring, nothing catastrophic is going to happen. Too often however, we find ourselves in defensive or apologetic positions that increase the members' discomfort. Or, because of our anxieties, we intervene too soon in the group process, conveying messages of concern, disapproval, or defensiveness. Or, even worse, we communicate the message that the members are incapable of handling the problem without our assistance. By remaining calm it gives us time for observation and data collection and a chance to determine exactly what–if anything–to do.

Exploring Differences

Typically during periods of conflict, points of view become polarized. Opinions and competing positions get expressed in an exaggerated tone of self-justification or outrage. There may be hyperbole, embellishment, and distortion resulting in other members feeling the need to take sides. During such moments it is essential that the various antagonists have the opportunity to state their concerns and to be heard by the other group members. It is usually to the group's advantage that the issue move from a subset of members to the group as a whole. While inviting other members to share their observations and perceptions may lead to conflict escalation, it also increases the possibility of greater member objectivity.

In the heat of the moment, members quickly lose perspective as to the issues being discussed. A result is the raising of extraneous side issues and the group getting off track. We can get seduced into the conflict and lose our objectivity. By consciously maintaining a degree of distance, we are better able to keep the members on track, and reduce the possibility of finding ourselves forced into joining one side of the conflict or the other.

Affirming Conflict

It is essential that the worker demonstrates the ability to tolerate, and in fact, welcome the anger and frustration of group members. When this occurs, members are free to engage in a more free-flowing emotional exchange in which a wide variety of feelings and reactions can be explored and dealt with. To affirm conflict, however, we must understand our own tolerances of anger and conflict– both historically and in the present moment. Looking at our experiences historically means knowing how we have responded in the past to such elements as confrontation, disagreement, anger, or loud voices. While for some workers such behaviors and actions have relatively little effect, for others the response is debilitating anxiety.

Understanding our tolerance for conflict in the moment means tuning into oneself as the conflict is occurring and assessing our personal comfort level. For example, are we scared as to what is going on? Do we feel under attack? Are we feeling out of control? We also need to be mindful of our body language. Are our arms crossed? Have we pulled our chair back from the group? By having such self-knowledge both historically and in the moment, we are less prone to respond in a reactive mode–either overreacting or underreacting to the group's dynamics.

Monitoring Communications

Because of the potential for misunderstandings in small groups, the worker must be alert both to what is being communicated (said) and what is being received (heard). This means assisting members to understand each other by giving and receiving messages that are reliable and accurate. Summarizing, clarifying, focusing questions, and encouraging active listening are important worker interventions. Two indispensable tools that are available to the worker are process statements and "I" statements.

Process statements are used when the group is in danger of getting off track (e.g., scapegoating, or blaming or attacking a person) and for helping the members own what they are talking about and taking responsibility for their actions. Examples of worker process statements are the following: (1) I sense a great deal of frustration in the group right now. Rather than deal with it openly, it sounds as if you want to ignore the problem; or (2) I'm unclear as to what is going on. Would someone take a risk and tell us what you see as occurring in the group?

"I" statements are expressions of personal responsibility. Instead of talking about "we," "the group," "one," or "you" the speaker is encouraged to own his or her feelings, observations, or personal reactions. When the group interaction takes the form of "I" statements, a foundation is laid for members to assume responsibilities for their lives as well as their actions.

Confronting Constructively

The worker needs to be prepared to provide direct, constructive confrontation when appropriate. The objective is to help particular individuals and/or the group as a whole take responsibility for their actions and make sufficient commitments to consider changes. Confrontation may range in impact from a light challenge to a direct collision. When done effectively, it invites a member to examine his or her behavior and its consequences more carefully. Unfortunately, when done poorly, it can threaten the client and the group, engendering defensiveness, resentment, and alienation.

Remaining Nondefensive

Particularly when confrontation is directed toward the worker, he or she needs to be flexibly persistent and not strike out in return. It is particularly important that workers demonstrate interest in receiving and understanding negative feedback and show willingness to learn from it, when appropriate. It is also vital that we avoid the seductive trap of dropping our leadership responsibilities, responding to the challenge to become "just another member."

The most natural response to being attacked emotionally is to strike back in kind. No matter how good it might feel at the time, it is seldom productive. The worker is well advised not to react with an intensification of rules or authoritarian or judgmental statements. Nor should the issues be trivialized or ignored. A leader who is able to work through an attack without being destroyed or retaliating is able to provide a model for the members in handling aggression. It also provides the lesson that aggression need not be punitive or destructive.

Perhaps under these circumstances when conflict is all around us, the best advice for the worker is to take a few deep breaths, recognize the inevitability of the process, and repeat the mantra of "this too shall pass."

SUMMARY

When properly managed, conflict can serve as the catalyst for a range of positive effects. It can cause problems to surface and be dealt with in a group, clarify varying points of view, stimulate and energize members, motivate the search for creative alternatives, provide vivid feedback, create increased understanding of one's conflict style, and extend the capacities of group members. Conflict can also have negative outcomes including reduced cooperation, trust, and motivation. The goal for the worker is to reduce the negative results, while increasing the positive ones.

The members often recreate in the group the very problems that plague and defeat them in their daily interactions. Through the group experience, members are able to expand their awarenesses and acquire new skills. Worker strategies in dealing with conflict include establishing norms early in the group, affirming conflict as a group variable, remaining calm when there is conflict, exploring differences of opinions, monitoring communications, remaining non-defensive when challenged, and confronting group members prudently and constructively.

BIBLIOGRAPHY

Atkinson, Donald (1995). *Counseling diverse populations.* Madison, WI: Brown & Benchmark.

Bond, J.R. and Vinacke, W.E. (1961). Coalitions in mixed sex triads. *Sociometry, 24:*61-75.

Chu, J. and Sue, S. (1984). Asian/Pacific Americans and group practice. *Social Work with Groups,* 7:23-36.

Danesh, Hossain (1977). The angry group. *International Journal of Group Psychotherapy, XXVII:*59-65.

Edelwich, Jerry and Brodsky, Archie (1992). *Group counseling for the resistant client: A practical guide to group process.* New York: Lexington Books.

Egan, Gerald (1970). *Encounter: Group processes for interpersonal growth.* Belmont, CA: Brooks/Cole.

Eskilson, A. and Wiley, M.G. (1976). Sex composition and leadership in small groups. *Sociometry, 39*(3):183-194.

Festinger, L. (1957). *A theory of cognitive dissonance.* Palo Alto, CA: Stanford University Press.

Frank, Jerome (1955). Some values of conflict in therapeutic groups. *Journal of Group Psychotherapy, VIII* (2):142-151.

Hansen, James, Warner, Richard and Smith, Elsie (1980). *Group counseling: Theory and process,* 2nd ed. Boston: Houghton Mifflin.

Hocker, Joyce and Wilmot, William (1991). *Interpersonal conflict,* 3rd ed. Chicago: Nelson Hall.

Kormanski, Chuck (1982). Leadership Strategies for Managing Conflict. *Journal for Specialist in Group Work, VII:*112-118.

Leong, Frederick (1992). Guidelines for minimizing premature termination among Asian American clients in group counseling. *Journal for Specialist in Group Work, 17*(4):218-228.

Lumsden, Gay and Lumsden, Donald (1993). *Communicating in groups and teams: Sharing leadership.* Belmont, CA: Wadsworth.

MacKenzie, K. Roy (1990). *Introduction to time-limited psychotherapy.* Washington, DC: American Psychiatric Press.

Mitchell, Rex and Mitchell, Rie (1984). Constructive management of conflict in groups. *Journal for Specialist in Group Work, IX:*137-144.

Nicholas, Mary (1984). *Changing in the context of group therapy.* New York: Brunner/Mazel.

Reid, Kenneth (1991). *Social work practice with groups: A clinical perspective.* Pacific Grove, CA: Brooks/Cole.

Sarri, Rosemary and Galinsky, Meada (1967). A conceptual framework for group development. In R. Vinter (Ed.), *Readings in Group Work Practice.* Ann Arbor, MI: Campus Publisher, pp. 72-94.

Strachey, J. (1934). The nature of the therapeutic action of psychoanalysis. *International Journal of Psychoanalysis, XV:*127-159.

Tannen, D. (1990). *You just don't understand: Women and men in conversation.* New York: William Morrow.

Thomas, K. and Kilmann, R. (1974). *Thomas-Kilmann Conflict Mode Instrument.* Tuxedo, NY: XICOM.

Tuckman, B. (1965). Developmental sequence in small groups. *Psychological Bulletin, 63*:120-399.

Unger, Robert (1990). Conflict management in group psychotherapy. *Small Group Research, XXI*(3):349-359.

Worchel, Stephen, Coutant-Sassic, Dawana, and Wong, Frankie (1993). Toward a more balanced view of conflict. In S. Worchel and J. Simpson (Eds.), *Conflict between people and groups: Causes, processes, and resolution.* Chicago: Nelson Hall, pp. 76-89.

Yalom, Irvin (1995). *The theory and practice of group psychotherapy,* 4th ed. New York: Basic Books.

Chapter 6

Research and Groups:
A Mutual Aid System?

Alice Home

Groups and research have often been viewed as incompatible. Many researchers hesitate to use group-based data collection techniques because they are unsure how to manage possible bias. Similarly, group workers often resist doing evaluative research because they are concerned about how the results will be used, or because they lack research skills and relevant instruments (Galinsky and Schopler, 1993). Can research and groups form a "mutual aid system?" This chapter argues that group-based methods can enrich research, while monitoring group practice can strengthen professional effectiveness and credibility. Furthermore, when group work practitioners and researchers work together, each can benefit from the specific expertise of the other.

This chapter presents two approaches to combining groups and research. The first involves using focus groups as a means of enhancing the practical relevance of survey research, while the second uses self-assessment methods to analyze group practice. The principles of each approach will be presented and illustrated by an example from the author's research-practice experience.

ENHANCING RESEARCH
THROUGH GROUP TECHNIQUES

Discussion groups are used in social work practice and education to improve decision making. A well-functioning group can produce comprehensive and creative solutions that reflect the diverse opinions and experiences of its members. However, the very qualities that make groups productive can also limit their usefulness as research tools. Group influence can shape members' behavior thereby producing good individual and collective outcomes, while interaction allows spontaneous sharing of experiences and ideas. Yet, both influence and interaction can result in some members' contributions being heard and valued more than others', so that the final outcome may not fully reflect the group experience. For researchers, this means group-based data collection can produce biased results.

Researchers have sought to glean some of the benefits that group data can bring while reducing the risk of bias. They developed three group-based data-collection techniques. The first two impose strict controls on interaction and influence rather than make full use of group process. Both the Delphi and Nominal techniques seek to tap the opinion of groups of people with expertise in a given area, with a view to identifying zones of convergence and divergence.

In a *Delphi "group,"* the members remain anonymous and do not meet. Rather, members provide individual written responses to several open questions, then clarify, revise, and react to repeat summaries of their grouped ideas until either consensus or stability is achieved. The *Nominal technique* is helpful when a rapid solution is needed for a complex problem. While group members do meet, interaction and influence are tightly controlled so it is a group in name only (Lauffer, 1982). Members of these heterogenous groups write individual responses to specific questions. Each response is recorded and posted for all to see, and each point is clarified to ensure shared understanding by all participants. Usually, there is no interaction prior to the final priority-setting vote, but some groups allow members to discuss results of a preliminary vote before making a final decision (Mayer and Ouellet, 1991).

Both techniques ensure all participants have an equal opportunity to have their ideas heard, such that the final results take the full range of members' opinions into account. However, the strict control of group process also limits their potential to enhance research. The third approach is a type of group interview, which seeks to make use of interaction and influence rather than to eliminate them. Focus groups are short-term, homogeneous groups of 6 to 12 people, who reflect on a limited number of questions in the context of others' views. This process allows the group to weed out extreme views while focusing on the most important issues (Patton, 1990). The one- to two-hour discussion is either taped or notes are taken by a recorder, while a second person facilitates the group. The quality of the data depends on question clarity, facilitator skill, and the quality of thematic content analysis (Morgan, 1988).

Focus groups can be used as primary, self-contained data-collection instruments, or in conjunction with interviews, surveys, or participant observation (Morgan, 1988). Using focus groups as complementary data allows researchers to compensate for weaknesses in other data-collection methods, by triangulating or cross-checking different data sources against each other (Denzin, 1978). For example, workers who had referred stressed families to a respite care service completed a questionnaire regarding impact of the service on child placement. They then participated in a group interview, during which they reflected on the overall effects of the service (Home and Darveau-Fournier, 1995). Focus groups can be used at various stages in the research process: at the beginning to deepen sensitivity to key issues or to develop relevant instruments, or at the end to reflect on the meaning of the results.

The use of focus groups as a complementary data source is illustrated by the author's survey research on multiple-role women studying social work, nursing, or adult education. This subject was chosen because increasing numbers of social work students are either employed or carry family responsibilities and many combine all three roles (Lennon, 1991). This study followed up on the researcher's earlier exploratory work, which found that students with three roles experience intense role demands and chronic role strain, and they receive mainly informal rather than institutional support (Home, 1993).

Nearly 500 students in 17 Canadian university programs participated in the survey. The goals were to investigate the relationship between role demands (expectations from each role), role strain (overload, conflict, and contagion), stress, and support. The researcher wanted to find out if any specific groups of multiple-role women were at higher risk for stress or strain and to identify any institutional supports that might reduce vulnerability. In many respects, this survey shared (Home, 1993) the advantages and disadvantages of all quantitative-descriptive studies that examine relationships between variables (Tripodi et al., 1985). However, this study was supported by a strategic grant,* which stipulated that results should be made available to a wide audience of potential users, including policymakers. The researcher was aware that academic research results are shared primarily with a limited number of fellow researchers and then only at the end of the project. Consequently, the potential impact on policy and practice is limited.

The researcher decided to use an adapted focus group format to reach out to a wide audience of potential research users. Four regional feedback sessions were planned early in the data analysis process so that practitioners, instructors, policymakers, employers, and students could reflect on preliminary results, trace policy and practice implications, and suggest action strategies. Participants' feedback was to be added to survey results to produce a summary pamphlet for multiple-role women and those who teach or work with them. This material would also be used in a handbook to be distributed to selected policymakers, employers, and community groups interested in improving the situation of multiple-role women.

A general format was developed for the first session, then revised slightly based on evaluation results. The classic focus group format was adapted to address the dual goals of complementary data collection and dissemination. While focus groups are usually homogeneous, these groups were composed of invited educators, community group and union representatives, and practitioners and policymakers from social work, nursing, and adult education settings. Unlike the typical focus group that is done entirely in small groups, the feedback sessions also included an introductory presentation and a closing plenary led by the researchers. The hour-long focus group portion allowed participants to explore either workplace or educational implications. These group sessions were followed by a

*This study was supported by a grant from the Strategic Grants Division, Social Sciences and Humanities Research Council of Canada. Cora Hinds (School of Nursing, University of Ottawa) was co-investigator, while the Canadian Association of Schools of Social Work and the Canadian Association of University Schools of Nursing were partners in this research.

short plenary, during which recorders summarized main points for discussion and final decision making by all.

Experienced group facilitators led each group, using written guidelines that were explained in a brief training session. A recorder took notes, as it was felt audiotaping might inhibit some participants from speaking freely. Each group warmed up with members highlighting which results were most relevant for their educational institution or workplace, then the groups considered three questions. They identified policies or practices that supported multiple-role women in their institutions or workplaces, they noted obstacles to setting up effective supportive measures, and recommended strategies for regional and national action.

One recommendation was to distribute regional summaries to participants, who were to find ways to share them with others in their universities, colleges, associations, or workplaces. Accordingly, summaries were distributed, not only to the hundred-plus participants in the four sessions, but also to invited others who had been unable to attend. Subsequently, thematic content analysis was carried out, using Miles and Huberman's (1984) coding, data display, and analysis techniques. This analysis allowed data to be grouped and summarized by question theme, while identifying both regional and professional similarities and differences.

Using adapted focus groups was a successful strategy for enriching this survey research and for enhancing its practical relevance. First, rich qualitative data was obtained, which allowed researchers to understand and explain the survey results more fully. For example, one student who ran between her part-time job, her elderly mother, her children, and her studies said she learned nothing about nursing the first year. But she learned to study in little bits of time, to drive in all kinds of weather, to survive on little money, and to work despite lack of sleep. She brought alive the concept of role overload and showed that many women cope despite tremendous obstacles.

A second advantage of using focus groups was that many more people had a chance to hear and reflect on results than would have been the case if the researcher had limited dissemination to traditional academic conferences and articles. The data were available not only to feedback-session participants, but also to a wide and varied audience who were sent copies of the short, readable summary pamphlets and handbooks. After summarizing the survey data, these documents focused on practical implications for target groups. For example, the pamphlet advised multiple-role students to join together for mutual support and social action, while suggesting that instructors and colleagues recognize the heavy load these women bear and work toward making existing policies and practices more flexible. Similarly, the handbook emphasized that "combining employment, family and education is a growing trend" and that "finding creative ways to adapt" to this new reality would help individuals and their institutions prepare for the twenty-first century (Home et al., 1995, p. 10). The handbook then outlined partnership and cooperative strategies that employers and educational administrators could consider to increase options for multiple-role women.

USING RESEARCH TO IMPROVE GROUP PRACTICE

If groups can be used to enrich research, is the reverse also possible? The second part of the research-practice interface is using research to monitor and improve our practices with groups. This is a controversial subject. On the one hand, professionals are being required to justify their decisions, to be explicit about what they do, and to prove their effectiveness (Alter and Evens, 1990). Social workers are seen as having responsibility to offer clients only those interventions that have proved effective; thus, monitoring practice is viewed as essential to maintaining professional credibility (Grinnell and Siegel, 1988). However, some workers fear that evaluation results could be used to eliminate jobs, while others argue practice is too complex to evaluate (Alter and Evens, 1990). Measurement problems are compounded by group workers' uneven research skills, by the lack of relevant instruments, and by the need for research designs that offer flexibility yet provide adequate control of individual, group, and contextual variables.

Social work has tried to deal with these dilemmas by developing the practitioner-researcher model, which emphasizes similarities between research and practice while inviting workers to do both in their daily work. Single-subject designs are of particular interest, because the practitioner-researcher can monitor change over time by making repeated assessments of an individual or a group (Alter and Evens, 1990). This approach is not without limits, however. Results cannot be generalized, bias is difficult to control, measurement is often restricted to quantitative assessments of behavior, and many workers find they barely have enough time to lead groups let alone evaluate them. Situating practice-research in a field placement context and using a flexible approach to measurement, however, make it possible to get around some of these difficulties.

An example is a master's-level field placement in which a student set up, led, and collected data on a group of French-speaking adult adoptees who were searching for their birth families (Rochon, 1994). The primary group goal was to offer an opportunity for sharing and mutual helping in the participants' own language. In addition, this project was viewed as an action-research experience, in which members and worker could reflect on needs and available services and action strategies, such as forming an ongoing French-language self-help group. This project drew on several group work models. Some self-help group features were present, as the worker was an adult adoptee who shared relevant life experience with the members' group. The mainstream social group-work model predominated, however, in that the worker had a clear but gradually diminishing leadership role focused on fostering mutual aid and empowerment (Papell and Rothman, 1983). The group had only six biweekly meetings, because of members' time commitments coupled with the relatively short (four-month) field placement. A variety of program activities were used to address key themes, as shown in Table 6.1.

The research component also featured diversity, with five research questions and several research instruments as shown in Table 6.2. A pregroup interview guide was used both to prepare the group and collect data on members' needs and uses of services. Participant observation was used to collect data on group meetings, using a tape recorder and notes. Finally, a group-administered questionnaire was developed as a self-report tool to assess the usefulness of the group in meeting goals and to estimate perceived satisfaction with the group and its various components. A verbal group evaluation was also done, so that individual and group results could be

TABLE 6.1. Program of the Adoptee Group*

THEME		PROGRAM
Meeting 1	Getting to know each other, identifying expectations	• exercise in dyads • group discussion
Meeting 2	Reconstructing our origins	• identifying baby pictures • identifying sources of members' talents
Meeting 3	Dream vs. reality: experiences with the search process	• small- and full-group discussion of members' needs and experiences during the search process
Meeting 4	Impact of adoption and the search process on loved ones	• group discussion with resource person
Meeting 5	Dream vs. reality revisited: what helped us?	• group sharing regarding usefulness of services/resources • discussion of a possible reformed group
Meeting 6	Usefulness and future of this group as a resource	• discussion of group's contribution • decision about reforming it • celebration with invited loved ones

* Adapted and translated version of table 2, Rochon (1994), p. 28.

TABLE 6.2. Summary of Research Method Used in Adoptee Group*

RESEARCH QUESTIONS	DATA-COLLECTION PROCEDURE
1. What needs are identified by adult adoptees who are searching for their birth parents?	• (pregroup) interview • participant observation (meeting #3)
2. What resources/services are used in the search?	• interview, observation (meeting #5)
3. To what extent did these resources/services meet needs?	• interview, observation (meeting #5)
4. To what extent and in what ways did the group meet individual needs?	• observation (meeting #6) • group-administered questionnaire (post-group)
5. a) Which needs are still to be met? and b) What strategies are suggested for meeting them?	• interview, observation (meeting #6) • group-administered questionnaire

* Adapted and translated version of table 3, Rochon (1994), p. 35.

compared through source triangulation (Denzin, 1978). Content analysis was carried out in order to reduce, organize, and describe data.

This project demonstrated that single-subject designs can be integrated into group practice in a creative way. However, it was not easy for the worker to facilitate the group while simultaneously being an observer. Similarly, while her dual role of member-leader deepened her understanding and empathy, she sometimes had difficulty knowing when to share her own adoptee, search, or reunion experiences without overinfluencing the others (Rochon, 1994).

This practice-research approach produced high-quality, rich data in response to all research questions, but the data regarding the group's usefulness are of particular interest in this chapter. Not only did the results point to the often cited need to share with others "on the same wavelength" who want to be "accepted in their difference" (as adoptees), but the data also identified useful program activities (Rochon, 1994). For example, discussing where members' talents and interests came from helped them to sort out the respective roles of environment and heredity, while sharing past or present search and reunion experiences helped members feel less alone and be more realistic in their expectations.

Assessing the group's impact also pointed to some planning problems that would need be addressed prior to offering similar groups. Consistent with self-help traditions, this group was heterogeneous as regards members' stages in the search process, but one member whose reunion had taken place ten years previously felt her needs had not been met. Secondly, despite enthusiasm about continuing on a self-help basis with new members, this group was not able to follow through and become an autonomous group. Building empowerment and autonomy takes time and requires a specific program to address leadership skills. A six-session format simply did not allow members time to develop both the confidence and the skills needed to take over the group.

CONCLUSION

This chapter has discussed and illustrated two approaches to making research groups mutually beneficial. Neither approach is without its difficulties and limits, but both hold promise as ways of reducing the gap between research and practice while enhancing group workers' capacities to do both. It is hoped that group work practitioners and researchers will experiment with some of the ideas in this chapter and report on their experiences.

REFERENCES

Alter, C. and Evens, W. (1990). *Evaluating your practice: A guide to self-assessment.* New York: Springer.

Denzin, N. (1978). *The research act,* 2nd ed. New York: McGraw-Hill.

Galinsky, M. and Schopler, J. (1993). Social group work competence: Strengths and challenges. Paper presented at the 15th Annual Symposium for the Advancement of Social Work with Groups, New York.

Grinnell, R., Jr. and Siegel, D. (1988). The role of research in social work. In Grinnell, R., Jr. (Ed.), *Social work research and evaluation,* 3rd ed., Itasca, IL: Peacock, pp. 10-21.

Home, A. (1993). The juggling act: The multiple role woman in social work education. *Canadian Social Work Review,* 10(2):157-182.

Home, A. and Darveau-Fournier, L. (1995). Respite child care: A support and empowerment strategy for families in a high-risk community. *Prevention in Human Services,* 12(1):69-82.

Home, A., Hinds, C., Malenfant, B., and Boisjoli, D. (1995). *Managing a job, a family and studies: A guide for educational institutions and the workplace.* Ottawa: University of Ottawa.

Lauffer, A. (1982). *Assessment tools.* Beverly Hills: Sage.

Lennon, T. (1991). *Statistics on social work education in the United States: 1991.* Alexandria, VA: CSWE.

Mayer, R. and Ouellet, F. (1991). *Méthodologie de recherche pour les intervenants sociaux.* Boucherville: Gaëtan Morin.

Miles, M. and Huberman, M. (1984). *Qualitative data analysis.* Beverly Hills: Sage.

Morgan, D. (1988). Focus groups as qualitative research. *Qualitative research methods,* number 16. Newbury Park, CA: Sage.

Papell, C. and Rothman, B. (1983). Le modèle du courant central du service social des groupes en parallèle avec la psychothérapie et l'approche de groups structuré. *Service social,* 32(1/2):14-29.

Patton, M. (1990). *Qualitative evaluation and research methods,* 2nd ed. Newbury Park, CA: Sage.

Rochon, J. (1994). *Partager et profiter de l'expérience des autres: Un groupe pour adultes adoptés francophones.* Mémoire de maîtrise inédit. Ottawa: École de service social.

Tripodi, T., Fellin, P., and Meyer, H. (1985). *The assessment of social research,* 2nd ed. Itasca: Peacock.

Chapter 7

Bullying and Scapegoating in Groups: Process and Interventions

Hisashi Hirayama
Kasumi Hirayama

An interpersonal phenomenon known as "bullying and scape-goating" in groups has long been a concern of group workers, family therapists, and teachers. A survey, conducted by Hirayama and Alissi (1992) on 83 group workers in the New England region, reports that 59, or 71 percent, of the respondents said they had scapegoats in their groups and experienced difficulties in handling the problem. Over the years, much has been written about this subject matter by group workers (Garland and Kolodny, 1976; Shulman, 1967, 1992), family therapists (Bell and Vogel, 1960), and small group theorists (Cartwright and Zander, 1960; Levine, 1979). However, this group phenomenon is attracting renewed interest among group workers, teachers, and parents because of at least two recent phenomena in societies like Japan and the United States. In Japan there have been several incidents of suicidal deaths of junior high school students whose motives were attributed to their experiencing severe bullying by their classmates. In the United States, sharply increased violent activities by youth gangs have emerged as a major societal problem. In these gangs, such behaviors as aggression, intimidation, threatening, bullying, and scapegoating are frequently used as the means to keep members in line with their organizational hierarchy and structures.

In this chapter, we will revisit this group phenomenon, bullying and scapegoating, by reviewing the literature to identify a process of social role assumption and assignment, to tease out interventions

89

that are known to be effective and could be utilized by group workers, and also to consider preventative measures.

First, we would like to tell you about an episode we witnessed in the ancient city of Kyoto, Japan, on a bright summer afternoon. When we were crossing a small bridge over a ravine in a small park, we heard a little commotion under the bridge, so we looked down. We saw that five or six school-uniform-clad teenage girls were hitting, with clenched fists, the face of another girl, taking turns one-by-one. The girl was screaming with pain and begging for mercy, but the battering continued until we commanded them to stop. We demanded they identify their school, because we wanted to report this incident to the school authorities. But our command was unheeded and no one responded. Then, in the next moment, one-by-one the girls started to retreat into the wooded area and disappeared. Next we witnessed a most amazing scene. The abused girl also followed the retreating group and disappeared from our sight. Since the girl's behavior was contrary to our expectation, we were simply dumbfounded. But we realized at that moment that the abused girl was a vital member of the group who assumed the scapegoat role in the group.

According to the dictionary, bullying is defined as "to intimidate with superior size or strength," and a "bully" is "a person who is habitually cruel especially to smaller or weaker people;" a scapegoat is defined as "one that bears the blame for others," or "one that is the object of hostility" (*Webster's*, 1985). Shulman (1992, p. 442) defines the scapegoat as "a member of a group who is attacked verbally or physically by other members." He further explains that "the scapegoating idea goes back to an ancient Hebrew ritual. Each year, on the Day of Atonement, the chief priest would symbolically lay the sins of the people in the form of a goat's skin (scape) on the back of a live goat and then drive the goat over a cliff. The death of the goat led to the ritual cleansing of the sins of the people" (p. 442). This custom was worldwide; the Jewish people were unusual only in being content to offer the life of an animal, for in many other places, the scapegoat was human. The Athenians, for example, kept a reserve of such outcasts, and each spring drew from it one man and one woman and stoned them to death. On the Niger, the two victims were bought with the fines of those who had sinned. On this scale, in 1858, grave sinners such as thieves and witches paid about two English schillings apiece toward the cost of the human sacrifice (Bronowski, 1955).

History has witnessed whole populations, such as African Americans, Japanese Americans, Jewish people, Hispanics, and gays and lesbians, who have experienced extreme forms of scapegoating as part of systematic oppressions. These forms have included the projection of negative stereotypes as an underlying justification for slavery, such as sending Japanese Americans to concentration camps by depriving of them of their constitutional rights as American citizens; and anti-Semitism and the Holocaust in which millions of Jewish people as well as many homosexuals, Gypsies, and the mentally and the physically disabled were systematically killed. Shulman (1992) says, "The idea of oppression as an expression of the oppressor's insecurity (as well as economic self-interest, etc.) . . . can help to explain the scapegoating process in a group." (p. 442) This general insecurity is expressed in the form of misplaced anger, frustration, hatred, and revenge against the scapegoat, while the majority assume the role of bully or oppressor. Our thought is that once the bully and scapegoat role relationship is developed, it usually forms a pattern and becomes a ritual. While selected members of the oppressor group may actively engage in oppressive activities, the majority remain as silent bystanders, implicitly condoning the violence inflicted upon the victims, and they later claim ignorance or innocence. The bullying and scapegoating phenomenon is not only an intragroup but also an intergroup phenomenon.

FUNCTIONS OF THE SCAPEGOAT

The functions of the scapegoat have been identified and described from psychological, organizational, and sociological perspectives. Erich Neumann (1969) explains the scapegoating phenomenon as a manifestation of projecting a negative part of one's unconscious psyche. He calls this "the projection of the shadow," and says, "the shadow, which is in conflict with acknowledged values, cannot be accepted as a negative part of one's own psyche and is therefore projected—that is, it is transferred to the outside world and experienced as an outside object. It is combated, punished, and exterminated as 'the alien out there' instead of being dealt with as 'one's own inner problem'" (p. 43). From an organizational perspective, Joan Lartin (1988) describes a scapegoating phenomenon in a hospital as follows:

> An example of scapegoating is the nurse manager who is extremely disorganized, working in a somewhat chaotic nursing department. When she exhibits this behavior, she becomes an excellent candidate for assuming the scapegoat role. Her peers and members of the administration may decry her disorganized style but they do not tell her that organization is a standard for being a nurse manager. This nonintervention and behind-the-scenes criticism combine in such a way that it is easy for this nurse manager to bear the "sins" of an entire department. Another form of scapegoating occurs when the leader of a group fears the group's anger or frustration. The leader focuses blame on a scapegoat in an effort to deflect the group's anger. Used chronically, this maneuver buffers the leader from negative experiences, but still prevents the resolution of the underlying problem. (p. 25)

Lartin further discusses a number of factors or conditions that contribute to the process of scapegoating in health care settings. They include high levels of anxiety or stress; an inability or unwillingness among the staff to recognize their own weaknesses; an institutional culture that promotes the notion that organizational or unit problems are one person's fault (the presence of a staff member who seems to provide realistic reasons for blame); and leaders who are very sensitive to criticism (Lartin, 1988).

Bell and Vogel (1960) have described the dynamics of the scapegoating phenomenon in the family group, emphasizing the functional role played by the scapegoat in maintaining equilibrium in the family by drawing all of the problems to himself or herself. Others have seen this phenomenon as a sadomasochistic relationship that satisfies the needs of both tormenters and scapegoats.

In summary, the scapegoat functions in a variety of roles. Bullies project onto the scapegoat their own negative feelings about themselves. The scapegoat role is often interactive in nature, with the scapegoat fulfilling a functional role in the group.

INTERVENTIONS

A wide range of interventions has been suggested for group workers, therapists, teachers, and parents to solve the problem of scapegoating. However, because of the absence of empirical evidence, there still is a shortage of interventions proven effective in preventing and alleviating the bullying and scapegoating phenomenon. Because of their psychoanalytical leaning, most earlier publications show biases toward interventions targeted either onto a scapegoat or scapegoaters, while relatively little attention has been paid to group dynamics or the interaction between the scapegoat and the scapegoaters.

We will briefly review interventions commonly utilized by group workers, therapists, teachers, and parents who frequently experience the scapegoating phenomenon in their day-by-day activities.

Garland and Kolodny (1976) have identified a range of 12 commonly used interventions. We will describe here only those we consider significant.

Squashing

Probably this is the most frequently used tactic by unsophisticated social workers, teachers, and parents to stop scapegoating by children. Squashing is immediate and strong reprimands. Garland and Kolodny (1976, p. 71) remark, "Scapegoating behavior may be stopped by moral sanction and threats and permitting no other consideration." For instance, as an aftermath of the suicidal death of a junior high school student, an immediate preventative measure was adopted by the school and the PTA–"squashing" students' behaviors. A result was increased tension in the school. One student commented to a newspaper reporter, "Our little horse play invites severe reprimands from teachers who are overly sensitive and reactionary. The entire school is full of unbearable tension" (*Asahishinbun,* March 6, 1995). Squashing on the surface appears effective, but it merely drives the problem underground and increases tension, resentments, and guilt among group members.

Protection

Protecting the scapegoat is a commonly used tactic. Protecting a weak, abused, and tormented victim is virtuous, morally acceptable behavior on the part of the worker. But its drawbacks are not in solving the problem but in pushing it underground, alienating the majority, and creating resentment. The only time this intervention is needed is to prevent serious physical harm that would otherwise be inflicted by bullies.

Diversion

Finding another outlet, either through physical activity (bowling, sports) or by using another person as the target, offers a diversion. The latter may be the worker himself or herself, or at times, generalized "outsiders" (boy or girl friends or ex-spouse). This is a temporarily helpful measure, as it does not deal with the "real" issues underlying group interactions.

Reducing Interaction

Another frequently used method is reducing opportunities for interaction by providing structure or activity to cut down contagion, stopping meetings to provide a cooling-off period, or limiting the lengths of meetings to preclude blow-ups. This is effective as a stop-gap measure, although it does not provide a permanent solution.

Ego Support

Garland and Kolodny (1976) consider ego support to be one of the most desirable methods that provides solutions to the problem. They state that "via skill training, and so on, ego support may be provided" (p. 71). The purpose is "making attackers more secure, stronger, and less in need of 'pecking'" (p. 73) the scapegoat. This position is based on the notion that scapegoating is a result of projection and displacement of "powerless egos of members, where issues of autonomy and competence are at risk." They conclude that "Workers are tempted to throw their energies into dealing with obvious attack phenomena and to protect the underdog. What is needed is confidence on the part of the worker to intervene instead into the background issue of bolstering self-confidence through help in developing activity skills or acquiring autonomy through making decisions about group affairs." (Garland and Kolodny, 1976, pp. 71, 72).

Ego support is perhaps most akin to the contemporary concept of empowerment. But one distinctive difference is that the concept of ego originates in individual psychology and is applicable only to understanding individual behavior and personality in a group; it is not an appropriate concept to explain group phenomena. The rest of the techniques described by Garland and Kolodny (1976) are ones that "make the scapegoat hardier, more competent in his own eyes and in the eyes of the group" (p. 73). We found limitations with all of these techniques, as they are focused on the individual.

Larry Shulman (1992), based on the interactional approach, views the issue of bully-scapegoat from a different perspective. He takes the position that bullying and scapegoating is a phenomenon of role assigning and role assuming in groups, not something inherent in particular "personalities" of individuals. This means that whether a person, or a group of people, becomes a scapegoat depends on interactions, a result of unique and complex interactions created in particular circumstances. Acknowledging that scapegoating is a phenomenon emerging out of interactional processes, the worker must focus on the process of interaction, which produces changes in the role relationship between the scapegoat and the bullies.

Furthermore, Shulman (1992) observes that the issue of scape-goating may arise more frequently in an earlier stage of group formation. He also observes that when group members scapegoat another member, they usually attack the aspect of the other that they most dislike in themselves, and that "one should think of this process as a form of communication to the worker of the group members' feelings about themselves" (p. 456). Shulman (1992) concludes that, in working with the scapegoating pattern, the worker must take a number of steps to seek a solution:

1. The worker should observe the pattern over time.
2. The worker must understand his or her own feelings in the situation to avoid siding with or against the scapegoat. By tuning in skill, the worker can attempt to search out the potential connections between the scapegoat and the group. If the worker is not clear about these connections, the group can be asked to reflect on what they might be.
3. This involves pointing out the pattern to the group and the scapegoat. Thus the worker asks the group to look at its way of working and to begin the struggle to find a more positive adaptive process. The two thrusts of the worker's efforts involve asking the group to consider why they scapegoat and also asking the scapegoat to reflect on reasons for volunteering for the role.

Now let us turn to the ways in which 59 practicing group workers responded to the question of how they had handled the problem of scapegoating in their groups (Hirayama and Alissi, 1993). The following summarizes how they had handled targeting the scapegoat and targeting the group as a whole.

Targeting the Scapegoat

1. Encourage assertiveness and promote self-protection.
2. Intervene to stop scapegoating. Leave it alone once arrested without further interference with group process.
3. Intervene later to involve scapegoat's expression of feelings and opinions.

Targeting the Group as a Whole

1. Redirect–point out to the group what seems to be going on. Discuss it.
2. Help the group to solve the problem, confront the group with the issue. Make it a group issue, lead members to talk about effects and perceptions. Point out to the group what the worker sees happening. Check with the person being scapegoated: how was he/she feeling and what did he/she want to do?
3. Encourage members to help that member (the scapegoat), and encourage the scapegoat to confront the group.

4. Discuss with individuals targeting the scapegoat how to explore their feelings and actions in a very supportive atmosphere.
5. Shift group attention from negative relatedness and communication to positive ones. Suggest other methods rather than scapegoating.
6. Point it out in a combination of gentle but direct feedback: can the person understand how she or he got into that position?
7. Confront—ask the group about their role in keeping that person scapegoated so attention and focus is off themselves.
8. Talk about behaviors and patterns of response that get them into this position. Ask people to claim responsibility for the issue being projected onto one member.
9. Deal with differences as strengths of the group and the individual. Also encourage group members to share how they are different.
10. Reflect feelings; switch roles (role plays) and change physical arrangement of space.
11. Reframe the content away from individuals to the group. Encourage the group to come up with solutions and talk about their experiences of scapegoating.
12. Redirect focus from the scapegoat to the members involved, helping them to understand how that person feels and to refocus to own issues. Make the issue clear to the group and discuss it. Encourage the group to explore ways to deal appropriately with what is occurring.

Data have shown that the overwhelming majority of the group workers surveyed appear to be very aware of the problem involved in bullying and scapegoating in groups. Furthermore, with a few exceptions, the majority of their intervention efforts are directed to the group process rather than targeting the scapegoat or the bullies, as the group workers seem to view scapegoating as a group phenomenon, rather than a manifestation of individual "personality" weakness or deficiency.

PREVENTING SCAPEGOATING

While there are no guarantees that scapegoating can be prevented, there are some preventative measures that the group worker can take. One of the most important measures is to maintain open communication with members (Lartin, 1988; Shulman, 1992). Analysis of several severe scapegoating incidents in Japan indicate the absence of open communication between the teacher and the students. As a matter of fact, those teachers whose students committed suicide had no inkling of the problem with bullying and scapegoating among their students until these tragic deaths occurred. To the extent that a climate of openness is fostered by the group worker, members will be free to air their problems as they are encountered rather than letting them fester or by scapegoating others. Open communication–people saying what is on their minds to each other–can be difficult, particularly in a society like Japan, where a sensitive, indirect communication style is regarded as preferable to a direct and open style of communication. However, the ability to address issues directly, openly, and matter-of-factly is a learned skill; role modeling by the group worker increases the probability that members will learn to follow suit.

A second strategy for preventing scapegoating is to develop an environment or standard that discourages members from complaining to anyone, including the group worker, except to those with whom he or she has the complaint (Lartin, 1988). In other words, the group worker lets it be known that members are expected to speak to the person directly concerned. It is critical that the group worker provide a role model for others. "I think you need to speak with A" is a simple yet powerful method of modeling this expectation (Lartin, 1988). The group worker strives to create "a system of mutual aid" in the group, and speaking directly and openly to each other is an important step toward creating a cohesive group where a sense of mutuality will be fostered.

A third way to decrease the likelihood of scapegoating is to be tolerant of individual differences (Lartin, 1988; Shulman, 1992). The group worker must send a clear message, verbally and nonverbally, to members that we live in a culturally, ethnically, and racially diverse society and a world where none of us is exactly alike. Differences in persons should not be interpreted as weaknesses or deficits in character or personality.

A fourth way to decrease the likelihood of scapegoating is to develop community levels of interventions by targeting various community groups, such as school, neighborhood, and ethnic groups in the community. This strategy may be carried out within a practice frame of community development in which the prevention of intra- and intergroup scapegoating becomes one of the goals for community organizers and community workers. Currently, most of the social group-work literature focuses on intragroup functioning, roles, process, and skills (Goldberg-Wood and Middleman, 1990). Despite the claim that social group work finds its roots in the Settlement Movement, a form of community development, the general direction of social group work in the past has been in the form of individual-focused practice, more or less "therapeutic" than self-development or prevention (Mayadas and Elliott, 1995). Despite repeated calls to develop community-level interventions, so far insufficient efforts have been exerted by group workers. Our intent here is not to consider possible solutions to the problem, but rather as a beginning effort, to identify some group-work skills that may be transferable to community practice. Applicable skills include communication skills, such as mediation, negotiating, bargaining, and conscientization; action skills of advocacy, empowerment, adaptation, change, and solidarity; and finally, analytical skills of assessment, and evaluation of functioning, process, and outcome (Mayadas and Elliott, 1995). We can possibly put these skills into a conceptual package of what Mayadas and Elliott call Social Development Systems.

CONCLUSION

We believe that bullying and scapegoating are complex processes in any level of human interaction and are generated and sustained by many contributing factors. While scapegoating ostensibly solves some problems in the short run, it invariably creates more serious ones in the long run. Group workers are in a unique position to prevent or to change this process when it threatens to interfere with morale and the individual and group's well-being. Perhaps all that is required is an effort for members to be genuine, open, and accountable to each other rather than permitting a scapegoat to "bear the sins" of others (Lartin, 1988).

REFERENCES

Asahishinbun (Asashi daily paper) (1995). March 6.

Bell, N.W. and Vogel, E.F. (Eds.) (1960). *A Modern Introduction to the Family.* New York: Free Press of Glencoe, pp. 382-397.

Bronowski, J. (1955). *The Face of Violence.* London: George Braziller.

Cartwright, D. and Zander, A. (Eds.) (1960). *Group Dynamics,* 2nd ed. New York: Harper & Son, pp. 25-29.

Garland, J.A. and Kolodny, R.L. (1976). Characteristics and resolution of scapegoating. In S. Bernstein (Ed.), *Further Explorations in Group Work: Essays in Theory and Practice.* Boston: Charles River Books, pp. 55-74.

Hirayama, K.K. and Alissi, A. (1992). A survey of group work practice in the New England region. Unpublished manuscript. West Hartford, CT: University of Connecticut School of Social Work.

Lartin, J. (1988). Scapegoating: Identifying and reversing the process. *Journal of Nursing Administration,* 18(9):25-31.

Levine, B. (1979). *Group Psychotherapy: Practice and Development.* Englewood Cliffs, NJ: Prentice Hall.

Mayadas, N.S. and Elliott, D. (1995). Developing professional identity through group work: A social development systems (SDS) model for education. In M.D. Feit, J.H. Ramey, J.S. Woodarsky, and A.R. Mann (Eds.), *Capturing the power of diversity.* Binghamton, NY: The Haworth Press, Inc., pp. 89-107.

Middleman, R.R. and Goldberg-Wood, G. (1990). *Skills for Direct Practice in Social Work.* New York: Columbia University Press.

Neumann, E. (1969). *The Scapegoat Psychology: Depth Psychology and a New Ethic.* London: Hodder & Stoughton, pp. 43-51.

Shulman, L. (1967). Scapegoats, group workers, and pre-emptive intervention. *Social Work,* 12(2):37-43.

Shulman, L. (1992). *The Skills of Helping Individuals, Families, and Groups,* 3rd ed. Itasca, IL: F.E. Peacock, pp. 441-467.

Webster's Ninth New Collegiate Dictionary (1985). Springfield, MA: Merriam-Webster.

Chapter 8

Helping Long-Term Homeless Men Regain Their Personhood Through Social Group Work

Janet S. Elder

BACKGROUND

Homelessness has been a social issue throughout the history of our country. However, the dramatic increase in the homeless population in the 1980s brought this issue to the foreground for society once again. We know that the current causes of homelessness are lack of affordable housing, gentrification, lack of educational opportunity, and a change in our society from a manufacturing-based economy to a service-based economy, to name a few.

The value system of our society provides a very different picture of homelessness. It is based on the beliefs of the majority populations' adherence to American cultural values. This value system emphasizes high individual achievement, responsibility for one's problems, emotional self-containment, hard work as a virtue–"success is both the path to and evidence of salvation" (McGill and Pearce, 1982).

The result of our societal adherence to this value system has moved the issue of homelessness from the structural realm to the personal realm. The homeless are characterized, labeled, and stigmatized as the disaffiliated, disempowered, passive, isolated, addicted, or mentally ill misfits in our society (Goldberg and Simpson, 1994).

INVOLVEMENT WITH OTHERS

Although homeless men are often together in large groups, e.g., waiting in line to eat, sleeping in shelters, and in day centers, they have little involvement with others except at the most superficial level. They report while living at the survival level that they cannot trust anyone, and although they form temporary alliances with other homeless men to achieve goals, these alliances end when the goal is achieved.

For example, if a client is "staying out," he may form an alliance with another client to "watch his back" while he sleeps. These men take turns sleeping and "watching each other's backs." Then they may move on or this arrangement may continue for a period of time. This strategy is necessary on the street in order to stay alive, as life on the street is very dangerous. Sometimes these men will also form an alliance to roll another homeless person who has a coat or a bottle of wine, work a street corner panhandling, or rob weaker homeless men at the first of the month when the disability checks come out. All of these alliances are temporary, and the man who watched your back on Monday may rob you on Tuesday.

Life on the street is very violent and as one client says, "trust can get you killed." Sexual alliances occur in much the same framework as nonsexual alliances. There is little or no sexual intimacy on the street. There is little privacy. Many sexual encounters, for both men and women, are violent, impersonal, and often involve prostitution or rape. Sex becomes a medium for getting survival needs met, getting money for drugs and alcohol, or for a place to get in from the elements. Sex is also a medium of power on the street. Weaker men as well as women are often raped.

As I spoke with these men individually, several common themes emerged. They all expressed a need for something to do, some place to go, and money to do it with. They indirectly expressed the need for safety, both physical and emotional, and for acceptance and dignity. Out of these interactions came the idea to form a group with a recreational format to address some of the needs presented by the men. The recreational format was chosen because this format directly addressed the spoken needs expressed by the men, and they viewed recreation as nonthreatening. The group modality would offer opportunities to meet the nonverbalized needs of the men: safety, dignity, and acceptance. The men were willing to try this idea although they were very skeptical about the process and questioned that the group would be successful from the outset. Because they have few choices in their lives, the group activities were chosen by the men, not by me. This process of choosing the group activities was initially done by consensus in the group. That process soon became difficult and cumbersome. I proposed turntaking to the group and they liked it very much. Each week one man would decide on the activity for the group, the menu for the meal, or choose the restaurant.

Initially, only two men came to the group. The agency did not have any place for a group meeting so we decided to make a group room. With the agency's permission we cleaned, painted, and furnished a room in the basement for a group space. As that work progressed, more men began to come to attend the group. The group room became very significant to the group members because they had created a space that belonged to them and they had played an important part in its creation. They had a place to be, they belonged.

Because they are alone and isolated in their life on the street, the group modality offers a place to practice and learn skills, and to give and receive mutual aid and social support that they lack in their everyday lives. For example, at one group meeting the clients expressed that they would like to use the group time to visit two agency clients who were hospitalized. Both men were near death from their alcohol abuse and living on the street. We visited the men, encouraged them to cooperate with the doctors, and invited them to the group when they were discharged. Both men joined the group after their discharges from the hospital. During their stays in the hospital, the families of these men had been contacted. The men had had no contact with their families for 5 and 11 years respectively. The family contacts were tenuous but positive. During the next four months, the group became an active support system for these men and a place where they could talk about their fears and desires regarding this family contact. All of the men in the group had been estranged from their families for many years, too. For most of the summer months, part of the group meetings were devoted to talking about, advising, and supporting the two group members in their reconnections to their families. By the end of the summer, both of the new members had returned home to make new beginnings with their families. Other group members had initiated contacts with their families and were actively working on repairing their relationships.

Another choice for a group activity in this time period contributed to the cohesiveness and self-esteem of the group members. The group decided to take a canoe trip as an outing. It was supposed to be a seven-mile trip and take about four hours. There were seven men and two social workers. What was planned to be an idyllic paddle down a stream out in the country turned into a nine-and-a-half-hour outward-bound activity. We had been told that the river was a little low and that we would have to portage the canoes in a couple of places. A couple of places turned into four and a half miles of portage. We were exhausted, dirty, wet, and sore at the end of the trip. The experience created an almost visible change in the men. None of them knew they could do that. Conquering the difficulties, pulling together, encouraging and supporting each other, working as a team, and winning were very new experiences for them.

At the meeting the next week, I gave each man a certificate of achievement and we processed the events of the canoe trip. I particularly called attention to how hard the trip was for each of us as individuals and how important our support of each other had been. I suggested that because we were able to support, help, and work with each other, the trip, although difficult, had been a successful achievement instead of a disaster. The men agreed and we talked about the importance of working together and helping each other in this instance and about ways we could continue to help support each other every day.

DEVELOPING SKILLS

I found that the men in the group had many skills, a lot of knowledge about human behavior, and good problem-solving skills. For example, one of the men in the group worked and traveled with a carnival for many years. He has wonderful verbal skills so I asked if he would be willing to solicit some donations for the group. He said he would not do it because if he was turned down he would cuss the person out. I suggested that he practice with different group members representing different business owners. Reluctantly, he agreed as did the other group members. I outlined the format of the call and he decided what to say. He and the other members practiced and then he made five calls, getting donations from four people and one "maybe." Both he and the group members were elated by his success, which was really a success by the group as well as by the individual who did the soliciting. I said to them that they had all done a good job and we talked some about how each member had contributed to the process.

INCREASING SELF-EFFICACY

Bandura (1982) defines self-efficacy as referring to beliefs about one's ability "to produce and to regulate events in [one's] life" (p. 122). Development of self-efficacy for long-term homeless men begins with the decision to come to the group. This decision entails a conscious choice on the part of the client to begin to take charge of his life. Many long-term homeless men have difficulty carrying out a commitment to be at a specific place at a specific time. The choice to come to the group also entailed a choice for substance abusers. The agency does not allow the use of substances at the agency. However, because many of these men are unable to stop using without significant physical problems, we allow them to come to the group when they have been using as long as they are not disruptive, combative, or unable to participate due to their consumption levels. They may not use during the group time, however. Because they may use and come to the group, self-efficacy begins because they must begin to choose to moderate or control their substance intakes in order to be a part of the group. Some men have been very successful and others struggle quite a bit. If the men come to the group and are unable to participate due to their substance use, they have to leave, but are able to return the next week. There have been several occasions when men have used during the group: they were sent out if the group was at the office, or put in a cab at their expense if we were in the community.

The group has been involved in art projects; creating and maintaining a garden; gone on camping, fishing, and museum trips; gone to the movies, on picnics, bowling, etc. All of these outings have allowed the men to increase their self-efficacy in some way. Every successful outing has challenged their pictures of themselves as defective and unable to interact with mainstream society, and has resulted in enhancement of their self-efficacy. Even the outings that were problematic increased self-efficacy, because through discussion the men gained insights about themselves and their actions.

DEVELOPING A CRITICAL CONSCIOUSNESS

Developing a critical consciousness involves understanding how the personal is political.

The group has been a useful tool in combating these men's views of themselves. All of the men in the group have had the experience of being unable to successfully negotiate with the social service system. They have been thrown out of chemical dependency programs, banned from shelters, refused medical care, and have further integrated these experiences as proof of their defectiveness. Because the group structure necessitates that the men define the way the group operates, and because the activities are determined by choices made by the men, the group has been successful. This success challenges the idea that they cannot or will not participate in or are unable to use services.

Over the time the group has been in existence, we have had to change how the group functions in order to meet the needs of the men. Originally the group met for two hours in the morning. As the group went on, I noticed that some men were late and others left early almost every week. When I asked about what was happening, I found out that these men were either coming from or going to feeding stations. Because all of them were "staying out," the only way they got food was to go to the feeding stations at set times. After I found this out, I talked to the men and we decided to have a meal as part of the group and to expand the group to a four- to five-hour format. Choosing and helping to prepare the meal in the group has increased opportunities for choices as well as presenting new opportunities for group cohesion. Sometimes the men prepare the meal, sometimes I prepare the meal, and sometimes we eat out. When I prepare the meal, it is a way of nurturing the group members. When we prepare the meal together, it is doing-with-talk-on-top (Middleman and Goldberg-Wood, 1991).

At those times and when other opportunities present themselves, I will express the view that perhaps their lacks of successes in other programs stem from the programs' inabilities to meet their needs.

This is a novel thought for these men, as they have internalized the idea that they are the problem. However, as the group progresses, they have begun to look at the idea that the structure is at fault rather than themselves. It is a slow process but it is beginning to happen.

As they get more comfortable with having choices, the men have become more able to assess situations around the idea of "does it meet my needs" and "can I be successful (in that framework)." For example, when the group began, all of the men were homeless and were "staying out." Now, they all have moved into housing. However, when they first decided to come in, they would move into the first available living situations. Many of those situations were not workable for the men and the result was often evictions. Over time and through observing others in this process, the men have all moved into more suitable living arrangements. This process has occurred through discussions in the group, trial and error, and increased awarenesses of their own needs. Members now assess their moves more often based on costs, availability of services, transportation needs, safety of the neighborhoods, etc. They have also begun to assess social service programs in the same critical ways.

REFERENCES

Bandura, A. (1982). Self-efficacy mechanism in human agency. *American Psychologist*, 37:122-147.

Goldberg, E. and Simpson, T. (1994, October). Challenging stereotypes in treatment of the homeless alcoholic and addict: Creating freedom through structure in large groups. In A.S. Alissi (Chair), *Hartford Symposium, XVI Annual Symposium on Social Work with Groups*. Hartford, Connecticut.

McGill, D. and Pearce, J. K. (1982). British families. In Giordano, J , McGoldrich, M., and Pearce, J. K. (Eds.), *Ethnicity and Family Therapy*. New York: The Guilford Press, pp. 457-479.

Middleman, R. and Goldberg-Wood, G. (1991). Communicating by doing: Families in society. *The Journal of Contemporary Human Services*, March.

Chapter 9

Developing Social Skills Programs for Children with Emotional Disabilities

Juanita B. Hepler

Social interactions and involvement in play activities with peers are hallmarks of childhood. Children spend hours interacting with one another and adolescents are famous for their "endless telephone conversations." One reason children spend so much time in these activities is the sheer enjoyment they apparently derive from such interactions. Indeed, the child who is left out or who has no friends is frequently described as sad, depressed, and or even angry at being rejected. How do children with emotional disabilities fare in their social interactions with peers? One might surmise that they would experience difficulties because of their tendencies to use inappropriate behaviors, such as aggression. This appears to be the case, as a number of studies have documented that children with developmental disabilities are at risk for experiencing problems in their relationships with peers.

Some of the problems they encounter include the tendency for nonhandicapped children to play with other nonhandicapped peers and frequently exclude children with disabilities from their activities. Children with disabilities also tend to receive more negative behaviors from peers than nonhandicapped children. It appears that when there are positive social interactions, the nonhandicapped children may use more adult-like behaviors so that interactions more closely resemble those of adult-to-child rather than child-to-child. If this is a predominant pattern, children with disabilities would have fewer opportunities to practice those all-important child-to-child interactions so necessary for positive social development. Placement in special schools or classrooms further isolates these children and limits their opportunities to engage in "normal" play activities and to practice the use of effective social skills (Gresham, 1982; Guralnick and Groom, 1988; Ray, 1985; Taylor, Asher, and Williams, 1987).

Although placement in special schools or classrooms separates children with handicaps from nonhandicapped peers, mainstreaming does not appear to appreciably improve their social situations. Simply putting these children in the same settings with nonhandicapped children does not mean the two groups interact (see Gresham, 1982; Hepler, 1994b). In an earlier study with learning disabled children (Hepler, 1994b), it was found that the learning disabled children gave very positive ratings of their nonhandicapped classmates, indicating that they would like to play with them. However, the nonhandicapped children gave very low ratings to the learning disabled children, demonstrating that they were not inclined to interact with these children. These differences in the ratings of the two groups were statistically significant.

Another component that impacts on the social interactions of children with handicaps is their social skills deficits. Again, a number of studies verify that many of these children lack positive social skills. The use of more aggressive and inappropriate behaviors (which are particularly noted with children with emotional and behavioral disabilities), poor problem-solving skills, and the tendency to misinterpret cognitive cues have all been listed as problems that children with disabilities exhibit (Crick and Grotpeter, 1995; Guralnick and Groom, 1988; Hepler, 1994b; Plienis et al., 1987). The lack of opportunities and the tendency for interactions with nonhandicapped children to be negative may hinder the development of more sophisticated skills; in fact, Guralnick and Groom (1988) indicate that many children with disabilities perform well below their levels of cognitive development.

Based on the literature, then, children with emotional disabilities are likely to be restricted in their opportunities to interact with nonhandicapped peers, and when they do, the interactions are often negative. Furthermore, those in mainstreamed classrooms do not fare well, because nonhandicapped children tend to play with other nonhandicapped children and exclude those with disabilities. In this chapter, I discuss a social skills program that we conducted with a small group of children with emotional disabilities. I will describe our efforts to address the negative attitudes of peers and provide skill development for the children with disabilities.

IMPORTANCE OF SOCIAL INTERACTIONS

Anyone who has observed a child who is rejected by peers knows that this is extremely painful for children. In our own work, we have seen the sadness, frustration, and anger of children who are excluded. We have talked with parents who are concerned about the negative and sometimes hostile environments their children encounter in social interactions. Some children appear suicidal, and it is not surprising that poor peer relationships are often cited as a contributing factor in suicidal and substance abuse behaviors (see Kline, Canter, and Robin, 1987; Seigel and Griffin, 1983; Windle, 1990). A well-documented relationship exists between peer rejection and school performance, school drop-out, and juvenile delinquency (Kupersmidt, 1983; Kupersmidt, Coie, and Dodge, 1990; Parker and Asher, 1987). Peer acceptance in childhood apparently has long-term consequences and may impact on mental, emotional, and employment adjustment in adulthood (Ginsberg, Gottman, and Parker, 1986; Parker and Asher, 1987).

What occurs in children's activities with peers that make these activities so crucial to social adjustment? First, they provide children with an opportunity to learn and practice new social skills, and children who do not have the opportunity to acquire skills in early childhood are ill-prepared for the more sophisticated interactions of adolescence and adulthood (Hepler, 1995). In addition to specific behaviors, children also learn physical and cognitive skills from one another. These physical and cognitive skills are, of course, interrelated with social behaviors. Children learn social control and adapt to society's values as they engage in play activities. For example, temper tantrums have a very different affect on peers as opposed to parents. Parents may have to deal with the tantrum, but peers can simply exclude the child who demands special attention. When children insist on "fairness" when playing a game, they are incorporating society's value of "fair play." Children also provide support to one another that can be very beneficial when a child is experiencing stress, because peers live in the same world and understand the issues the child faces (Hartup 1983; Fine, 1981; Berndt et al., 1980). And, finally, when interactions are positive, children have fun; Gottman (1983, p. 74) describes complex play activities as "high adventure" and most of us can probably remember several high adventure episodes from our childhoods.

The negative consequences of peer rejection and the positive impact of interactions with peers are substantial and explain the concern of helping professionals for children who are experiencing difficulties in their social developments. The documented low status of children with emotional disabilities highlights their special needs. In our study, we attempted to address the two issues that impact on the social status of children with emotional disabilities: the skill deficits of these children, and the negative attitudes of nonhandicapped children toward children with emotional disabilities.

IMPLEMENTATION OF THE STUDY

This program was conducted at a daycare treatment center for children with emotional and behavioral difficulties who had been unable to make satisfactory adjustments in public schools. The agency provided schooling for grades one through six in a large metropolitan city in the northeast. Classrooms were small with five to six students in each class. All students were boys (the director reported that few referrals of girls occurred), which is not surprising as boys are more likely to exhibit disruptive behaviors in the classroom. The agency also provided intensive social work services to the children with two full-time social workers for 15 to 25 children. In addition, there were numerous aides and recreation staff who also worked closely with the children. The program utilized a behavioral approach including the use of tokens and rewards. All staff had been trained in the use of the model; consequently, it was systematically implemented throughout the agency, providing structure and stability for the children. A time-out room was used when children were unable to maintain self-control. An aide or staff member would sit with the child and help the child work through the issue so that the child could return to the classroom. Families were included in the program and given daily updates on their children's progress.

The goal of the agency was to work with these children and prepare them for eventual return to public schools. A child's stay depended on his or her progress. Some remained in the school for several years while others might return to public schools after three or six months.

As the reader might surmise, these children exhibited social skill deficits, especially in the areas of self-control and anger management. With rare exceptions, these children had very negative experiences in social interactions with peers in the public schools and most were apprehensive about returning to their former schools. The director and staff of the agency were concerned about the social skills deficits of the children and particularly concerned about the environments these children would experience when they returned to public schools. It was these concerns that prompted them to seek my assistance in implementing a social skills program at the treatment center.

The Social Skills Program

The social skills program consists of eight one-hour sessions that are specifically outlined in the social skills training manual developed by the author. For grades four through six, four behavioral skills (initiating and maintaining a conversation; including others; entering an ongoing activity; and responding to negative interactions from peers) and one cognitive skill (problem-solving skills) are taught in the sessions. Problems-solving skills consist of the ability to (1) identify the problem, (2) generate alternate solutions, (3) consider the consequences of each solution, and (4) select and implement the most effective solution. Several studies have demonstrated that these behavioral and cognitive skills are critical for positive social interactions with preadolescent youth (see Hepler, 1994a).

After a six-week training period conducted by the author, the two social workers at the center each led a social skills group in one of the fifth grade classrooms. I observed a number of the sessions and noted that the children frequently used inappropriate behaviors in the groups. These seemed to be accepted as normative behaviors by group members, although they would have drawn negative responses in a group of nonhandicapped children. At the conclusion of the eight weeks, student and staff assessment of the program was very positive; however, we had addressed only one of the components necessary for effective impact, namely, the skills deficits of the children. The second issue, improving the negative attitudes of nonhandicapped peers, had not been included in the program. As previously discussed, most of these boys had very negative experiences in their former public school settings. Their previous isolation and rejection by peers made them very apprehensive about returning to their schools, and their confidence levels were low concerning their abilities to interact with nonhandicapped peers.

At the time of this project, I was also conducting a social skills program in a suburban public school with fifth grade children with learning disabilities and nonhandicapped children. Each small group was composed of two children with learning disabilities who spent the greater part of each school day in special classrooms, and three nonhandicapped children. When the social workers from the day treatment center observed these groups and the positive interactions between the handicapped and nonhandicapped children, they enthusiastically agreed that their children would benefit from such an experience. In addition, the social workers saw what I had observed in the group sessions at the center, that is, they became aware of how severe the skill deficits of their children were. Because they worked with emotionally disturbed children only, they had come to accept some of their poor skills as normative. Observing nonhandicapped fifth-grade children showed them how much work needed to be done in order to develop the social abilities of their students. The social workers were impressed with the high level of social skills the children with learning disabilities exhibited in their groups with nonhandicapped peers. As a result of their visit to the public school, the staff at the center began planning for a similar program for their students.

Expanding the Program

The director of the treatment center approached a local elementary public school concerning the implementation of an eight-week social skills program that would involve four boys from the treatment center and six nonhandicapped children from the elementary school. The sessions would be held in the public school. The public school did refer children with emotional disabilities to the treatment center, and the director indicated that the social skills program would be a joint effort to prepare children from the center to make a smoother transition back into public schools. After several meetings with administrators, the school principal, and the helping professionals, an agreement was reached to implement the social skills program in the public school. The public school social workers, psychologists, and counselors were especially enthusiastic about the program. They were well aware of the negative social environments many of the children returning from the center encountered when they reentered public schools.

Prior to implementing the program, the public school social workers, counselors, and psychologists participated in training sessions with the author. When training was completed, we asked them to recruit members for two groups, emphasizing that they should be nonhandicapped children with high or at least average social status. We wanted higher status children so that the youth from the center would have a "safe" opportunity to interact with children who were accepted by peers and who exhibited a high level of social skills. These children would be excellent role models for children from the center, and interacting with high-status peers would improve their self-confidence. Permission letters were sent to parents of children selected to participate, describing the program and indicating that it would include children from the daycare treatment center and the public school.

The use of high-status peers was a crucial component of the program; however, when children arrived for the first session, it became apparent that two of the public school children who had been assigned to Group II had low social status and developmental disabilities. This had repercussions that will be discussed later. Group I was composed of two boys from the center, and two high- or average-status boys and one high- or average-status girl from the public school. One of the boys from the center was removed from Group I after the first week because the treatment center staff determined that he was not adequately prepared. Consequently Group I had three boys and one girl. Group II, as previously mentioned, had two low-status children (one boy and one girl) from the public school, one high- or average-status girl from the public school, and two boys from the center, for a total of five members (the higher status girl dropped out of the program after several weeks reducing the number of group members to four). Each group had two leaders: one social worker from the center and one social worker, psychologist, or counselor from the public school.

Group Processes and Outcomes

Group I and Group II met in separate rooms for the eight sessions. Students from the treatment center and the public school were very enthusiastic about participating in the program. Not surprising, the social workers from the center were somewhat apprehensive concerning their students' performances and behaviors in the sessions. Would they exhibit appropriate behaviors? Would the other children accept them? Would the experience cause extreme anxieties for their students? Except for the one boy who was removed, the three boys from the center remained very enthusiastic about the program throughout the sessions. When they returned to the center after the first session, they excitedly talked about their "experiences" with the other students. Several times they mentioned that there were girls in their group, a fact which seemed to raise the status of the two group members and the program itself. Other students listened intently as the boys recounted their very positive experiences in the sessions.

As all group leaders know, group composition has a major impact on group processes and group outcome (Sundel et al., 1985). This was clearly demonstrated in the social skills group. As pointed out, Group I had one student from the center and three high- or average-status public school students. The student from the center was particularly weak in social skills; however, he responded to the other children and their uses of appropriate behaviors. He did not exhibit many of the immature or inappropriate behaviors that he utilized at the center. Instead, he tried to emulate the skills and interactions of the public school students. Nor did he appear to have extreme difficulty using positive skills in an atmosphere where other children were relating in appropriate ways. Of course, it must be remembered that he felt he was in a relatively safe environment; that is, that group leaders would not allow interactions to become negative. The three students from the public school also enjoyed the sessions and appeared to take for granted that the student from the center would use appropriate behaviors. Based on my observations of the sessions and discussions with the two group leaders, the group was a positive experience for both the members and leaders. The leaders were able to cover the material including the behavioral and cognitive skills, and the children participated with interest and enthusiasm. The group leaders felt that the students did learn the skills emphasized in the program and that it had been beneficial for all members. At no time did any of the students from the public school indicate or even suggest that they would like to withdraw from the group.

Group II presents a somewhat different scenario. First, two of the three public school students were not average but low social status and had developmental disabilities. The young boy had severe behavioral problems and was apparently unable to adjust to the structure and constraints of a public school setting. The second student was a girl who tended to be quiet and withdrawn and lacked social skills. These two children were unable to serve as positive role models for the two boys from the center. The boy made it more difficult for the treatment center boys to maintain self-control, because he frequently used negative behaviors, and group leaders had to intervene. To their credit, the boys from the treatment center attempted to use appropriate behaviors even when the third boy was using inappropriate behaviors. The only high- or average-status member was a girl who appeared to have excellent social skills. After the first session, she became increasingly uncomfortable with the group. My assessment is that she determined that this was not a group she wanted to be a part of. None of her friends or more popular classmates were in the group. While the boys from the center recognized the inappropriate behavior of the public school boy, it did not damper their enthusiasm; however, the high-status girl was not impressed with the behavior and clearly did not want to be there. One of the counselors tried to encourage her to remain in the group, pointing out how beneficial her participation would be for the other members. When I was informed that she wished to withdraw from the group, I indicated that we should allow the student to withdraw, because no child should participate when they do not wish to. Furthermore, asking such a student to remain because she can help others does not contribute to developing the positive attitudes toward children with emotional disabilities that the program strives for. We are striving to promote the interactions between the two groups to a more equal level rather than one group helping the other. The remaining girl, who had been very quiet initially, became more involved as the sessions progressed and actively interacted with the boys from the center.

The group leaders had more difficulty leading this group. Inappropriate behaviors had to be dealt with and sometimes group progress was hindered, particularly by the boy from the public school. The leaders felt they worked extremely hard to cover the material in the manuals and to help students learn the new skills. My observation of the group confirmed their reports: the group was more unruly, progress was slower, and more was demanded of the leaders. Nevertheless, the four group members were very enthusiastic about the sessions and both the leaders and the students felt that the students had learned valuable skills.

Several measures were administered before (pre) and after the completion (post) of the program to assess the impact of the sessions. Sociometric measures asked students to rate how much they liked to play with fellow group members, the role-play test assessed their knowledge and appropriate applications of the specific cognitive and behavioral skills emphasized in the program, and observational data was collected to assess the quality of the social interactions within each group. While it is not within the scope of this chapter to provide detailed descriptions of the results, preliminary analysis shows that positive outcomes occurred in each group. At the final session, students were asked to evaluate the program. They were asked to rate how much they enjoyed the group on a scale of 1 to 5, with 1 being a very low rating and 5 indicating that "they enjoyed being in the program a lot." It also asked them to assess the value of each skill, if the specific steps taught for each skill seemed appropriate, and if they planned to use these skills. Again, results were positive. For example, seven of the students gave the sessions a rating of 5, and one gave a rating of 4. These are very high marks and we were extremely pleased that both the public school and treatment center children obviously enjoyed being in the program. It is also interesting that Group II, which may have had more difficulties, rated the sessions high; in fact, the 4 rating occurred in Group I. The staff from the treatment center felt that the experience improved the confidence levels of their students in their abilities to play with "other kids." It was a very rewarding experience for those of us who had worked with these children to observe their progress.

During the eight weeks of the program and the additional weeks in which we collected observational data, no issues arose with teachers, the principal, or parents, and while suggestions were made on ways we could improve the project, the response was positive. I believe this was the result of the careful planning by the public school and the treatment center staff. The preliminary meetings and training sessions were invaluable in preparing the staff. And finally, the cooperation of the families and children helped to make the program a meaningful, positive experience. Further support for the program and the methods was demonstrated by the public school. The following year, the social workers, counselors, and psychologists at the public school implemented the social skills program with fifth grade children, and again reported positive outcomes. While they were not necessarily working with children with emotional disabilities, they indicated that the groups included both high- and low-status children.

SUMMARY

In this chapter, I have discussed the importance of social skills and the problems children with disabilities encounter in their social interactions with peers. In working with this population, I have stressed two points: the negative attitudes of nonhandicapped children toward children with emotional disabilities must be addressed, and the skills deficits of children with emotional disabilities must be covered in the program. I have described the implementation of a social skills model that spoke to these issues. It required a great deal of planning and training but enabled us to bring children from the treatment center to a public school and provide them with a safe environment to practice and learn new skills and interact with nonhandicapped children. All children enjoyed participating in the program, but it was the children from the center who benefited most. For several of them it was probably the most positive experience they had ever had with nonhandicapped peers. That the public school continued to use the social skills program after completion of our project indicates that they felt the program was also very helpful for their students. This study demonstrates that agencies can work together to improve the social environments of children with emotional disabilities, and that the evaluation of outcome or the research component can also be conducted as long as the researcher is sensitive to the special constraints of schools. In this project, it meant working with the schools to find times for the sessions and administration of outcome measures that would cause the least conflict for the normal school schedule. It also meant modifying components of the program and research design so that excessive amounts of time were not requested.

The staff at the treatment center felt the social skills program, both at the center and in the public school, had been extremely beneficial for their students, and that the staff had increased their knowledge and sensitivity to issues of social development. The center provided me with additional funding to work with their students for another year. The focus for the following year would be on prevention, and would include intensive social skills training with the very young children (second graders). As previously suggested, the results of our work together demonstrate that agencies, practitioners, and researchers from academia can work together to address and have meaningful impacts on social issues that confront our people and society. While our endeavors were on a small scale, they clearly demonstrate the need and importance of such projects.

REFERENCES

Berndt, T.J., Caparulo, B., McCartney, K., and Moore, A. (1980). *Processes and outcomes of social influence in children's peer groups.* Unpublished manuscript. Yale University, New Haven, CT.

Crick, N.R., and Grotpeter, J.K. (1995, June). Relational aggression, gender, and social-psychological adjustment. *Child Development,* 66(3):710-723.

Fine, G. (1981). Friends, impression, management, and preadolescent behavior. In S. Asher and J. Gottman (Eds.), *The development of children's friendships.* New York: Cambridge University Press.

Ginsberg, D., Gottman, J.M., and Parker, J.G. (1986). The importance of friendship. In J.M. Gottman and J.G. Parker (Eds.), *Conversations of friends, speculations on affective development.* New York: Cambridge University Press, pp. 3-50.

Gottman, J.M. (1983). How children become friends. *Monographs of the Society for Research in Child Development,* 48(3).

Gresham, F.M. (1982). Misguided mainstreaming: The case for social skills training with handicapped children. *Exceptional Children,* 49(5):422-431.

Guralnick, M.J., and Groom, J.M. (1988). Friendships of preschool children in mainstreamed playgroups. *Developmental Psychology*, 24(4):585-604.

Hartup, W. (1983). Peer relations. In E.M. Hetherington (Ed.), *Handbook of child psychology* (Vol. 4). *Socialization, personality and social development.* New York: John Wiley & Sons, pp. 103-174.

Hepler, J.B. (1994a). Evaluating the effectiveness of a social skills program for preadolescents. *Research on Social Work Practice*, 4(4):411-435.

Hepler, J.B. (1994b). Mainstreaming children with learning disabilities: Have we improved their social environment? *Social Work in Education*, 16(3):143-154.

Hepler, J.B. (1995). Social skills training. In *Encyclopedia of social work*, 19th edition. Washington, DC: National Association of Social Workers, pp. 2196-2205.

Kline, R.B., Canter, W.A., and Robin, A. (1987). Parameters of teenage alcohol use: A path analytic conceptual model. *Journal of Consulting and Clinical Psychology*, 55:521-528.

Kupersmidt, J.B. (1983, April). *Predicting delinquency and academic problems from childhood peer status.* Paper presented at the Biennial Meeting of the Society for Research in Child Development, Detroit.

Kupersmidt, J.B., Coie, J.D., and Dodge, K.A. (1990). Predicting disorder from peer social problems. In S.R. Asher and J.D. Coie (Eds.), *Peer rejection in childhood*. New York: Cambridge University Press.

Parker, J., and Asher, S. (1987). Peer relations and later personal adjustment: Are low-accepted children at risk? *Psychological Bulletin*, 102:356-389.

Plienis, A.J., Hansen, D.J., Ford, F., Smith, S., Jr., and Kelly, J.A. (1987). Behavioral small group training to improve the social skills of emotionally-disordered adolescents. *Behavior Therapy*, 18:17-32.

Ray, B.M. (1985). Measuring the social position of the mainstreamed handicapped child. *Exceptional Children*, 52(1):57-62.

Seigel, L.J., and Griffin, J.J. (1983). Adolescents' concepts of depression among their peers. *Adolescence*, 18(72):965-973.

Sundel, M., Glasser, P., Sarri, R., and Vinter, R. (1985). *Individual change through small groups*, 2nd edition. New York: The Free Press.

Taylor, A.R., Asher, S.R., and Williams, G.A. (1987). The social adaptation of mainstreamed mildly retarded children. *Child Development*, 58:1321-1334.

Windle, M. (1990). A longitudinal study of antisocial behaviors in early adolescence as predictors of late adolescent substance use: Gender and ethnic group differences. *Journal of Abnormal Psychology*, 99(1):86-91.

Chapter 10

Group Work Education and the CSWE Curriculum Policy Statement: Capitulation or Coexistence?

Cyrus S. Behroozi

This chapter assumes that group work continues to represent knowledge and skills that social workers must possess in order to deal with practice imperatives that the profession faces. The importance of group work is based on its unique emphases on mutual aid, democratic participation, power sharing, and consciousness raising.

In spite of this importance, recent graduates of most social work master's programs have not been adequately prepared to practice group work. For example, of the social work master's programs recently surveyed, only six offered a concentration in group work (Birnbaum and Auerback, 1994). This problem is attributable to the curriculum policy statement of the Council on Social Work Education (CSWE), especially the ambiguity of its conception of social work practice in both the foundation and advanced components of the curriculum.

Thus, this chapter argues that the apparent decline of the importance of group work is directly related to the curriculum policy statement, discusses two primary responses to the statement, and identifies obstacles to group-work education beyond the issues represented by the statement.

TRANSFORMATION OF THE CURRICULUM POLICY STATEMENT

As stated by Greenwood (1957), there is a universal agreement that a primary attribute of any profession is a body of knowledge and skills necessary for achieving its purpose. Such knowledge and skills are acquired through required professional education and supplemented and updated through continuing education programs. The required professional education is defined according to standards formulated and monitored by appropriate professional organizations.

In social work, standards for the required professional education at the baccalaureate and master's levels are formulated and monitored by the CSWE Commission on Accreditation. The CSWE standards consist of two major components: eligibility and evaluative standards relative to such factors as educational program's faculty, administration, and financial resources; and standards for the baccalaureate and master's curricula set forth in the curriculum policy statement.

First published in 1952, the first curriculum policy statement defined social work practice in terms of casework, group work, and community organization. Since then, the statement has been transformed several times. The latest statement was approved in 1992. For the first time, the latest statement consists of two separate parts, one for the baccalaureate and one for the master's curricula in social work. This chapter focuses on the Curriculum Policy Statement for Master's Degree Programs in Social Work Education (CSWE, 1992).

Although the latest curriculum policy statement reflects a number of significant changes, it has reaffirmed the overall curriculum conception, which was published in the previous statement in 1988. Accordingly, baccalaureate social work programs are expected to prepare students for "generalist" practice through the "foundation" curriculum. In addition to the foundation curriculum, master's programs are designed to prepare students for "concentration" practice through the "advanced" curriculum.

In relation to the 1992 Curriculum Policy Statement for Master's Degree Programs in Social Work, while not explicitly stated, it can be assumed that the foundation curriculum is delivered in the first year and the advanced curriculum in the second year of the master's education. The 1992 statement consists of seven major parts (M1.0-M7.0) with 79 sections and subsections. Of these, 11 are introductory statements (M1.1-M3.7), 32 deal with the purpose of social work and the purpose and structure of master's education (M4.1-M5.8), 3 are in regard to the "liberal arts perspective" in the master's education (M5.9-M5.11), 2 are concerned with the overall master's curriculum

(M6.1-M6.2), 16 deal with curriculum content at the master's foundation level (M6.3-M6.13), 5 deal with field practicum at the foundation and advanced levels (M6.14-M6.16), only 5 deal with the advanced-level curriculum (M6.20-M6.24), and 5 are concerned with "avenues of renewal" (M7.1-M7.1.4). The first 43 sections and subsections primarily provide the context for the master's curriculum, and the other 36 serve as the specific requirements for various parts of the master's curriculum. As already stated, in the latest curriculum policy statement the foundation curriculum is expected to educate students for generalist social work practice, and the advanced curriculum is to prepare them for concentration practice.

The generalist-practice conception emphasizes the commonality and integration of social-work practice and, thus, has enhanced the identity of the whole professional practice (Papell and Rothman, 1986). However, this conception has given rise to a host of issues. To begin with, there is a confusion about the meaning of generalist practice. As concluded by Tolson, Reid, and Garvin (1994), not only does uniformity not exist about the meaning of generalist practice, but there is also a debate about whether generalist practice is a perspective or a methodology. In this respect, as Anderson (1983) has reported, another issue is that the term "generalist" (i.e., systemic) is confused with the term "generic" (i.e., universal). Furthermore, it is not clear whether generalist practice involves both direct and indirect practice or is merely another form of direct practice (Briar, 1976). The most pervasive conception of generalist practice is what Leighninger (1980) has called "skills generalist." Accordingly, the intent of this approach is "to discover those procedures and skills common across methods in such a way as to create a basic core of 'methods skills' applicable in work with individuals, families, groups, communities, and planning bodies" (p. 7). As such, ". . . all areas of social work practice [are viewed] as reducible to a series of basic steps or phases . . ." (p. 7). Leighninger has identified two major problems in this approach. The first problem is that in order to cover the wide range of social-work practice activities, the conception of skills generalist represents such broad levels of abstraction and generality that it becomes virtually useless as a guide to concrete action. The second problem is that, particularly in generalist conceptions attempting to utilize systems theory, there is an insufficient fit between theoretical framework and development of particular practice skills. Thus, although the conception of generalist practice may have some usefulness at the baccalaureate level, particularly in the field of rural social work, it can essentially serve only as a framework for practice at the master's level.

The latest curriculum policy statement has also reaffirmed the conception of concentration curriculum for the social work master's education. Furthermore, the statement has allowed master's programs the freedom to define their own concentration curricula in terms of any such frameworks as fields of practice, problem areas, population groups, contexts and perspectives, and intervention methods. The major issue here is that master's programs not choosing the intervention-methods framework may graduate advanced social-work practitioners who know much about problems and issues but not enough about how to deal with them effectively. Thus, particularly in relation to the concentration curriculum, the statement has diminished the importance of not only group work but also social work practice methodology in general.

As Kolevzon (1992) states, despite all the rhetoric, the standards and the curriculum policy statement represent a series of compromises in an effort to accommodate divergent and, at times, opposing interests in social-work education. These compromises have been particularly harmful to group-work education. In spite of the fact that group work continues to represent knowledge and skills that all social workers must possess in order to deal with practice imperatives that the profession faces, as reported by Birnbaum and Auerbach (1994), the master's education in social work has practically eliminated group work as a specialized area of study. They further report that coursework in social-work education includes little about group work and has limited or no fieldwork experience to develop group work skills. While the Birnbaum and Auerbach study was conducted in 1991, there is no indication that the 1992 curriculum policy statement in any way addresses this problem. At the same time, in many service fields, the need for competent practice with groups is rapidly growing because, among other reasons, it is assumed that group work is more economical than practice with individuals on a one-to-one basis. Consequences of inadequate group-work education in social work are serious for practice. These consequences include refusal of social workers to practice with groups because of their fears of failure, inadequate supervision of social workers who do practice with groups, and social workers' questionable imitations of other professions in practices with groups.

RESPONSE TO THE CURRICULUM POLICY STATEMENT

The problem of the inadequate group-work education in social work is attributable to the curriculum policy statement, especially the ambiguity of its conception of social-work practice in both the foundation and concentration components of the curriculum. Efforts by the Association for the Advancement of Social Work with Groups and others to remedy this problem in the latest revision of the curriculum policy statement led only to the retention of "systems" as the foci of social-work practice. Another significant effort has been the work of the association's Commission on Group Work Education. Such efforts should be directed at the improvement of the statement whenever it is reviewed for further revision. Meanwhile, in relation to the inclusion of group-work content in the curriculum, the response of social work master's programs to the statement can represent two primary options: capitulation or coexistence.

The response representing capitulation accepts the pervasive but problematic conceptions of generalist practice and concentration practice for the foundation and advanced components of the curriculum respectively. Accordingly, group-work content is "integrated" in generalist practice courses in the foundation component, and a few group-work courses may be included as electives in the concentration component. There is no evidence that such an approach prepares students for competent group-work practice upon graduation from master's programs. To learn how to practice with groups competently, students need to learn about the *process* of group work, which is distinctly different from other methods of social-work practice.

Within the context of the curriculum policy statement, the response representing coexistence defines generalist practice in the foundation component to include generic practice content as well as distinct courses on practice methods, including group work. To justify such an approach to curriculum development, let us examine requirements of the 1992 curriculum policy statement. In relation to the purpose of social work, the curriculum policy statement calls for the "promotion, restoration, maintenance, and enhancement of social functioning of individuals, families, groups organizations, and communities" (M4.1.1). Furthermore, concerning the purpose and structure of master's social-work education, the statement prescribes that all master's social-work programs must "provide content about social-work practice with client systems of various sizes and types" (M5.4.1). More specifically, in relation to social work practice content in the foundation curriculum, the statement requires the inclusion of "approaches and skills for practice with clients from differing . . . backgrounds, and with systems of all sizes" (M6.11). Consistent with these requirements, the foundation curriculum can include a generic practice course in the first semester followed by specific social-work practice-method courses, including a group-work course, in the second semester. To be useful in a broad range of social-work practice situations, such a foundation group-work course must include content on the use of groups for individual and interpersonal growth as well as for social action and organizational decision making. This kind of curricular arrangement clearly meets the requirements of the current curriculum policy statement and, at the same time, provides an opportunity for the development of practice competence in specific methods, including group work. Another approach has been proposed by Parry (1988) for the development of a foundation group-work course in a four-semester MSW integrative methods sequence.

In relation to the concentration curriculum, the curriculum policy statement is by far less prescriptive. In fact, as stated earlier, several examples of frameworks for the concentration curriculum are given by the statement, including intervention methods (M6.21). Considering this apparent ambiguity, the organization of the concentration curriculum in terms of practice methods, including group work, is both allowed and feasible. Accordingly, the concentration practice can be defined as a core of specialized, *selected* social-work method courses, including group work, built on foundation method courses. An example of this kind of advanced curriculum is defining concentrations in terms of interpersonal practice and macro practice. In the interpersonal practice concentration, a group work course can be one of the required courses along with courses on social work practice with the individual and with the family.

OBSTACLES TO GROUP-WORK EDUCATION

Why is such a coexistence with the curriculum policy statement not widely actualized? In other words, what are obstacles to the actualization of such a coexistence in social-work education? It seems that there are three interrelated forms of obstacles: obstacles on the part of group-work faculty, obstacles within schools of social work, and obstacles in the context of schools of social work.

The obstacles on the part of group-work faculty should be understood in relation to the decreasing number of such faculty in schools of social work. These obstacles include a perceived or real sense of powerlessness, absence of hope to bring about desired changes in social-work curriculum and instruction, and a possible lack of willingness or skills to bring about such desired changes.

As already noted, perhaps the most significant obstacle in schools of social work is the decreasing number of group-work faculty. In addition, there may be a lack of conviction about the importance of group work on the part of nongroup work faculty or a competition among them about various priorities. Another obstacle may be based on economic considerations, when offering fewer but larger courses seems more advantageous as compared with offering specialized but smaller ones, such as group work courses.

The obstacles in the context of schools of social work include "political" pressures represented by an emphasis on social problems and issues in social-work curriculum, even though strategies for dealing with these problems and issues are not adequately taught. In fact, such strategies may not be known yet, may not or cannot be effectively taught, or their implementation by social workers may not be possible for a variety of reasons.

These and similar obstacles are assumed to be contributing factors to the problem of inadequate preparation of group workers in schools of social work today. Therefore, while waiting for an opportunity to improve the curriculum policy statement, there must be an effort to examine these obstacles and to find ways for dealing with them.

REFERENCES

Anderson, J. (1983). Conceptual models of direct service generalist practice. Paper presented at the CSWE Annual Program Meeting, Fort Worth.

Birnbaum, M. and Auerback, C. (1994). Group work in graduate social work education: The price of neglect. *Journal of Social Work Education*, 30(3):325-335.

Briar, S. (1976). Generalist, specialist, and territory. (Editorial.) *Social Work*, 21(3):178.

CSWE (Council on Social Work Education) (1992). Curriculum policy statement for master's degree programs in social work education. Alexandria, VA: Council on Social Work Education.

Greenwood, E. (1957). Attributes of a profession. *Social Work*, 2(3):45-55.

Kolevzon, M. (1992). Should we support the continuum in social work education? No! *Journal of Social Work Education*, 28(1):10-15.

Leighninger, L. (1980). The generalist-specialist debate in social work. *Social Service Review*, 54(1):1-12.

Papell, C. and Rothman, B. (1986). Issues in education for social work with groups. Paper presented at the Annual Symposium on Social Work with Groups, Los Angeles.

Parry, J. (1988). Organizing principles for developing a foundation group work practice course. *Social Work with Groups*, 11(1/2):77-85.

Tolson, E., Reid, W., and Garvin, C. (1994). *Generalist practice: A task-centered approach*. New York: Columbia University Press.

Chapter 11

A Self-Directed Community Group
for Homeless People:
Poetry in Motion

Marcia B. Cohen
Julie M. Johnson

INTRODUCTION

Creative expression has long been associated with social group
work. The early settlement-house workers saw the arts as having
the potential to instill humane values (Addams, 1910), generate
understanding across diverse ethnic groups (Woods and Kennedy,
1922), and promote beauty and joy while educating people (Wald,
1934). Unfortunately, the relationship between the arts and group
work has considerably diminished in our generation as "poetry, the
visual arts, drama, music and dance have not been seen as especially relevant to social group workers . . ." (Getzel, 1983, p. 76).

Today, poetry is typically used in activity and expressive therapy
groups for such purposes as building self-esteem, improving communication skills, enhancing socialization, developing insight, managing anxiety, communicating with the unconscious, and facilitating the
expression of painful feelings (Bresler, 1982; Campbell, 1985; Gladding, 1987; Goldstein, 1989; Taylor, 1990). A review of the literature
on groups over the past 20 years suggests that poetry and other forms
of creative expression have largely been confined to treatment-oriented
groups. The review identified only four articles addressing nonclin-
ical uses of poetry in group work. Three of these articles discuss poetry
as a means of creative expression for groups of elderly people (Getzel,

1983; Koch, 1978; Rigg and Kazemek, 1987). Only one of these articles was written by a social worker. The fourth article (Kissman, 1989) explores the use of poetry groups in feminist social-work practice for purposes of empowerment, consciousness raising, and connection.

This chapter will discuss a poetry group developed in an agency for homeless and low-income people. The group was organized as a weekly workshop for people to come together and write about their lives. This was a task group, sharing some of the functions of empowerment and consciousness raising described by Kissman (1989) as well as a community education focus. Group goals, internal leadership issues, mutual aid, and the role of the worker in a self-directed (consumer-led) group will be explored as they evolved over the course of group development.

BACKGROUND AND ORGANIZATIONAL CONTEXT

The poetry group was developed by staff and service recipients in a nonprofit organization providing meals, clothing, and social-work services to homeless and low-income people in northern New England. The group grew out of the agency's weekly community meeting in which a number of service recipients expressed interest in a poetry writing group. The community meeting had previously been established as a self-directed task group (Cohen, 1994; Mullender and Ward, 1991a,b; Mullender and Ward, 1993) with the primary goal of increasing client influence in agency decision making. Once the poetry group had been requested through this forum, a grant to support it was written to and funded by the State Arts Commission.

The grant provided a stipend for a local writer to work with the group and also subsidized the subsequent publication of an anthology of the group's poetry. The group was developed and cofacilitated by the local writer and an agency social worker. The writer had considerable experience and long-standing interest in community organizing and political activism. The social worker had been involved in organizing the community meeting and was one of its cofacilitators. She had also worked on a community action project using street theater.

The design of the poetry group provided for member self-direction with the cofacilitators functioning in a consultative capacity. The agency's emphasis on empowerment, the facilitators' commitment to working with client strengths, and the client-driven nature of the community meeting that spawned the poetry workshop all influenced the formation of a highly self-directed group. Over time, this group evolved a stable structure, indigenous leadership, and mutually agreed upon goals that reflected participants' interests in self-expression, creativity, and community education about poverty and homelessness.

STRUCTURE AND COMPOSITION

The poetry group met weekly for over two years with attendance ranging from 5 to 15 members. It was an open membership group (Schopler and Galinsky, 1984) with a stable subgroup of seven core members. The core group included four women and three men, all white and between 25 and 55 years of age. All seven had been homeless. This core group included a higher proportion of women and middle-aged members than the larger agency population but reflected its predominantly Caucasian racial composition.

Members mostly used group meetings to write and share individual poetry and to compose group poems in which each member contributed a line of verse in a round-robin format. Meeting time was also used to plan community education activities, including poetry readings, speaking engagements at local colleges; and public appearances at block parties, state fairs, and arts festivals. For close to a year, planning for the publication of the group's poetry anthology was an additional group task.

The following group poem was written during a frigid New England winter:

Winter Dreaming

The windchill dropped to 40 below.
The wind howled and threw in snow.
My pile of wood in the corner seemed to be getting low.
Moving through the city, watching, in silence.
I wondered–What does life hold in the future?

The wind howled and brushed cold on my face.
I thought of sunbathing on the Fourth of July.
I wish my coat was warmer,
the wind feels like it is going through me.
It did and caught my soul, my life, my piety
and as I died, frozen, I felt my body rising,
Rising with the wind, rising as a light could in bright sunlight,
I looked the wind in the face and howled
and I danced and sang.
Then I woke up and remembered the dream I just had.

GROUP PURPOSE AND GOALS

From its inception, the primary group purpose was defined by members as artistic expression, rather than therapy or skill building. A secondary purpose was envisioned as educating the community at large about the homeless experience through the use of poetry as a vehicle for community action. During the initial phase of development, the following goals were negotiated and agreed upon: to meet weekly to write together, to organize poetry readings for the public, to publish an anthology of the group's poetry, to educate the public, to counter negative stereotypes about homeless people by giving voice to their experiences, and to communicate with similar groups around the country.

These goals were not arrived at easily. It was not uncommon for these group members to raise extremely personal issues in the middle of debates about local politics. The group became sharply divided over the inclusion of self-help content. Power and control issues dominated group meetings. During this period, the group's poetry often contained images of spirituality, which seemed to serve as a bridge from the personal to the political.

The cofacilitators helped group members understand their conflicts over goals as revolving, at least in part, around tensions between task and socioemotional content. Group members began to see the roles that personal expression and group interaction could play in enhancing their accomplishments of tasks. Examining group process and taking responsibility for working through disagreements enabled the group to clarify its goals while establishing norms for problem solving and decision making.

The group recommitted itself to its original purpose of creative expression and community education while becoming more tolerant about personal disclosure. Two participants who had been strong proponents of an enhanced clinical emphasis in the group made an unsuccessful bid for leadership and gradually stopped attending. The group moved into the middle phase of development with enhanced self-direction skills and increased cohesion. The function of promoting mutual aid in the group was shared by group members who increasingly saw themselves as comprising a community. The group had become intimately bound around its task.

An event from a mid-December meeting provides a good illustration of the group's ability to integrate task and socioemotional functions. The group was busy writing poetry for its soon-to-be published anthology when Betty arrived, in tears. Now in her 50s, Betty has experienced a lifetime of poverty and episodic homelessness. Although illiterate, Betty was a prolific poet.

On this particular wintery day, Betty had been informed by the Salvation Army that she was no longer needed to "work the kettles" at Christmas. She had worked for the Salvation Army in this capacity for many years and counted on the small income she received to buy Christmas presents for her daughters. Zeek, one of the younger members, suggested that they write a group poem about what had happened to Betty. As the poem was being written, Betty began to cry. Members of the group hugged her and offered their support.

The Bells

They silenced the bells today.
They told us not to ring them, anyway.
They want to "turn off" our voice.
Tell us "you ain't got no choice."
Shoppers don't want to think about the poor this time of year.
I guess this means we just should disappear.
I say "ring em loud, from the tallest high rise!"
Silence is no virtue, it's designed to cover lies.
I say "ring em loud, ring em proud."
So the people will know that there are poor on Christmas.

INTERNAL LEADERSHIP

Indigenous leadership roles were shared within the core group. Three of these members were also part of the internal leadership structure of the community meeting and were successful in transferring this status to the poetry group. These members were particularly interested in having the group serve as a forum for political education and advocacy. As discussed above, conflicts over group purpose and goals during the initial stage of group development resulted in two members making an unsuccessful bid for leadership. Following their departures, core group membership stabilized and a shared leadership structure evolved.

The workers reminded members of their status as facilitators and consultants, stressing that they were not the group's *leaders*. The self-directed nature of the group was continually clarified and tested (Mullender and Ward, 1991a). Core group members were helped to explore and accept the range of interests within the group as a whole. Many of the more sporadic group participants were attracted to meetings solely for the opportunity for self-expression and creativity. They looked to the group as a nurturing place for their writing. These participants were less involved in the group's community education activities.

Core group members carried the responsibilities of planning and implementing educational activities, working on the poetry book, and attending to group maintenance. Several core group members shared most of the task leadership functions while others fulfilled socioemotional leadership roles. Specific role assignments fluctuated and overlapped. Zeek, for example, often took on group maintenance roles in addition to providing considerable task leadership.

Zeek's poetry embodies the group's goal of raising public consciousness about homelessness. His poem entitled *Billy* is a powerful example:

Billy

When Billy turned 5 and started school the teacher asked,
"What do you want to be when you grow up?"
And these are the things that Billy didn't say:
"I want to be a junky and a dope addict.

I want to get married too young and beat my children and my wife.
I want to sell my body to perverts in the park
for twenty bucks or crack cocaine.
I want to live on welfare, food stamps,
and be a burden to my fellow man.
I want to beg for quarters
so I can buy some beer.
I want to sleep under bridges
and have young punks call me bum.
I want to stay in shelters
and slowly go insane.
I want to drink cheap wine
and puke and piss my pants.
I want to eat in dumpsters and soup kitchens
and smoke cigarettes that I find.
I want to be called lazy and shunned
by so-called gentlemen.
I want to smell of unwashed skin
and grow to hate my fellow man.
I want someone to kill me for the things I've become.
I want to be called a vagrant and a bum."
The things that Billy did say
are irrelevant because he's dead.
Killed by the hero of the town.

Lania, a young single mother, was another strong indigenous group leader as well as a prolific poet. Like Zeek, she infuses her poetry with social consciousness but her tone tends to be more personal. In *Changed Heart*, she describes her experience of falling from a middle-class existence where she "shooed" homeless people from the front steps of her business to a very different time when she was the one who was shooed away:

Changed Heart

Busy Busy!
Constant go!
Work busy!
Money blown!

Sign store!
Work profit!
Woman sitting
tired, nuisance
Shame, Shame!
Get out
Move on
Leave–Shoo!
Pissed, anger
Hurt, pain!
Different time
A different place
Still busy! Busy!
Constantly still going!
Now no work
Now no money
Divorce, lost children
Now I'm tired
I'm the nuisance
Get out!
Move on
Leave–shoo!
Pissed, anger
Hurt, pain!

COMMUNITY BUILDING THROUGH POETRY

Over time, the group evolved into a strong community of writers. Through poetry, group members voiced their common struggles as street people and survivors of the harsh realities of an unjust society. The group provided a safe and affirming place for people to share experiences and feelings, create poetry, and build strong bonds.

These bonds were strengthened further when the group took their show on the road. They began holding bimonthly coffeehouses featuring poetry readings open to the public. A fairly broad cross section of the larger community attended, including friends, families, neighbors, acquaintances, local artists, professionals, and students. The coffeehouses soon led to invitations to appear at other events around the state. A favorable article in the state's largest newspaper increased the group's visibility as did the publication of *Words from the Curb* (Preble Street Resource Center, 1994), the group's poetry anthology.

These opportunities to be heard by society's mainstream furthered the group's objective of community education through poetry. Members of the audience learned first-hand about the ravages of poverty, the pain and stigma of living on the margins, and the frequent losses and abuses associated with life on the streets. They were also introduced to the poets as resilient, competent, and creative individuals. Societal stereotypes of poverty and poor people were challenged, and myths about homelessness debunked.

An untitled poem from *Words from the Curb* (Preble Street Resource Center, 1994) reflects the social message of the poetry readings:

> We often take for granted
> the necessary and the true.
> We must wear clothes
> and the sky is blue.
> We live in a land that is free;
> not all do.
> We have cars
> and roofs above our heads;
> Some see only blue or black.
> If the sun is down and they
> can't turn on a star.
> That is, they have no home
> and their only food is
> an empty relish jar.
> Can such be in the land of the free?
> A great man once said, "If one
> in our land has no rights, no one does."
> We don't have a home
> merely a nation and a bill.
> Not only one man climbed a hill.

THE ROLE OF THE WORKER
IN SELF-DIRECTED GROUPS

From its inception, the cofacilitators saw the group as being member-led. They built on the empowerment-based model of the community meeting, which gave birth to the writers' group. This prior shared experience with self-directed group work helped the writers' group participants feel at home with this approach. The political consciousness and values of many group members, fueled by their experiences within homeless protest movements (Cohen and Wagner, 1992), was also highly congruent with a model that saw group members as being in charge.

Mullender and Ward (1991a,b; 1993) have provided a very clear and useful articulation of the worker's role in self-directed groups. They make a sharp distinction between the role of *leader,* which involves directing (controlling) the work of the group, and the role of *facilitator,* which is inherently nondirective. As facilitator of a self-directed group, the worker's primary function is to assist the group in discovering the means to achieve its own ends (Mullender and Ward, 1991a).

This nondirective facilitative role requires a complex application of group-work skills involving careful judgments and subtle nuances. The worker must be "directive about being non-directive," (Mullender and Ward, 1991a, p. 129), constantly navigating between the Scylla and Charybdis of overactivity and nonintervention. The degree of worker involvement will vary with the demands of the group but its nondirective focus must be consistent if the group is to be truly self-directed. The worker must be, at all times, alert, actively observing, and tuned into the "pulse" of the group in order to monitor its changing needs for worker intervention. The metaphor of a dance comes to mind. The worker's motions are flexible and fluid as he or she steps forward and back in harmony with group needs.

The cofacilitators of the poetry group were fairly successful in maintaining an active, nondirective stance. They saw their roles as highlighting group process (without trying to manage it), encouraging group members to identify and struggle with process issues, and creating an environment in which group members felt free to set their own goals. In doing so, these workers sought to embody Mullender and

Ward's suggestion that facilitators of self-directed groups draw out the "best from group members and [help] them determine where they want the group to go" (1991a, p. 129). The cofacilitators also functioned as consultants and resource people, using their professional knowledge (of community education, writing, book publishing) to advance collective community building and educational goals. In this context, the workers were acting as experts, but their expertise was placed at the group's disposal, rather than vice versa.

SUMMARY

This chapter has examined a self-directed, task-oriented poetry group whose goals emphasized creative expression and community education rather than therapy or skill building. Group members struggled with the need to balance task functions with group maintenance activities and discovered that the socioemotional dimension of the group could enhance task accomplishment and vice versa. The evolution of shared internal group leadership roles that integrated task and group maintenance functions proved instrumental to group functioning. Collective responsibility for mutual aid in the group evolved over time and was the glue that held the group together. Core group members' commitments to giving voice to the lives of homeless people, using writing as a vehicle for community education, and creating a place where service recipients could gather for the purpose of artistic expression, made the poetry group a vital and empowering force in the lives of its participants.

This group's emphasis on poetry as artistic expression *and* a vehicle for community education evokes group work's roots within the early settlement-house movement (Addams, 1910; Woods and Kennedy, 1922). This represents a new/old approach in group work, blending creativity, empowerment, and community action. As Jane Addams, Lillian Wald, and others discovered many years ago, art created in a group can be a powerful tool for community change.

REFERENCES

Addams, J. (1996). *Twenty years at Hull House.* New York: The Macmillan Company.

Bresler, E. (1982). Filling an empty universe: Poetry therapy with a group of emotionally isolated men. *Social Work with Groups,* 5(3):65-70.

Campbell, R. (1985). Writing groups with the elderly. In M. Sundel, P. Glasser, R. Sarri, and R. Vinter (Eds.), *Individual change through small groups,* 2nd edition. New York: The Free Press, pp. 556-559.

Cohen, M.B. (1994). Who wants to chair the meeting? Group development and leadership patterns in a community action group of homeless people. *Social Work with Groups,* 17(1/2):71-87.

Cohen, M.B. and Wagner, D. (1992). Acting on their own behalf: Affiliation and political mobilization among homeless people. *Journal of Sociology and Social Welfare,* 19(4):21-40.

Getzel, G.S. (1983). Poetry writing groups and the elderly: A reconsideration of art and social group work. *Social Work with Groups,* 6(1):65-76.

Gladding, S.T. (1987). The poetics of a "check out" place: Preventing burnout and promoting self-renewal. *Journal of Poetry Therapy,* 1(2):95-102.

Goldstein, M. (1989). Poetry and therapeutic factors in group therapy. *Journal of Poetry Therapy,* 2(4):231-41.

Kissman, K. (1989). Poetry and feminist social work. *Journal of Poetry Therapy,* 2(4):221-230.

Koch, K. (1978). Teaching poetry writing to the old and the ill. *Health and Society,* 56(1):113-126.

Mullender A. and Ward, D. (1991a). Empowerment through social action group work: The self-directed approach. *Social Work with Groups,* 14(3/4):125-139.

Mullender A. and Ward, D. (1991b). *Self-directed groupwork: Users take action for empowerment.* London: Whiting & Birch.

Mullender A. and Ward, D. (1993). The role of the consultant in self-directed group work: An approach to supporting social action in Britain. *Social Work with Groups,* 16(4):57-79.

Preble Street Resource Center (1994). *Words from the curb at Preble Street Resource Center.* Portland, ME.

Rigg, P. and Kazemek, F. (1987). All that silver: A poetry workshop in a senior citizens center. *Journal of Gerontological Social Work,* 10(3/4):167-182.

Schopler, J.H. and Galinsky, M.J. (1984). Meeting practice needs: Conceptualizing the open-ended group. *Social Work with Groups,* 7(2):3-19.

Taylor, J.W. (1990). The use of nonverbal expression with incestuous clients. *Family in Society: The Journal of Contemporary Human Services,* 71(10):597-601.

Wald. L. (1934). *Windows on Henry Street.* Boston: Little, Brown & Co.

Woods, R.A. and Kennedy, A.J. (1922) *The settlement horizon.* New York: Russell Sage Foundation.

Chapter 12

Social Group Work with the Elderly Mentally Ill: Beauty in the Beast

John L. Hart

The supervising nurse on the geropsychiatric unit once said, after reading a poem in which all the patients were being held in the belly of a beast, "I know what this means, I feel like this place is slowly eating all of us up too." The violence and fear and anguish on the units of a state mental hospital can be mind-numbing.

Strained state budgets have mandated that only the most violent, assaultive, and dangerous of individuals, those that are unacceptable for placement anywhere else, are housed at the state hospital. A growing part of the population are PCs, penal code patients. These are violent criminals who are physically and mentally incapable of coping with prison life and need skilled nursing care. One patient alone had 76 incidents of assaultive behavior toward staff and peers in one month. There is frequently at least one staff person per month who is in some way disabled from injuries caused by violent patients. "I'm going to kill you!" is something screamed out and heard nearly every day.

POETRY IN THE STATE HOSPITAL SETTING: "FRESH RED STRAWBERRIES"

Poetry writing and reading can bring some other kinds of language to the state hospital setting. "One of the important things that poetry can do is make us feel how our language works, make us feel good about words, and make words taste like fresh red strawberries on our tongue" (Doreski and Doreski, 1988). Making a place for poetry in the belly of the beast is a way of bringing some beauty and sensitivity and often some heart and soul into a dark reality. The great poet, Rilke, said about poetry, "There is only one single way. Go into your self" (Bly, 1990). The use of poetry for therapy has been in use for as long as poetry has existed. It is something that can hone and develop and nurture the senses. It stimulates imagination and spirit.

This can be essential in a place of violence and pain. The poetry can be something that can keep the senses alive. American poet Robert Bly said, "A human body just dead, is very like a living body except that it no longer contains something that was invisible anyway. In a poem, as in a human body, what is invisible makes all the difference" (Bly, 1990). Poetry in a state hospital setting can help make the difference in keeping the human spirit alive.

THE POETRY WRITERS' WORKSHOP GROUP

The Poetry Writers' Workshop group at Camarillo State Hospital began in the fall of 1994. The group met weekly on Tuesday mornings for an hour. The poets met in a pleasant, quiet room away from the noise and agitation of the geriatric unit dayhall. There was coffee, hot chocolate, or tea and occasional cakes and cookies.

There were usually one to three staff people involved—a therapist and two adult education teachers. Each staff person sat with three or four patients at a small library table. Each participant had notebook paper and a pen.

The new poets were new to writing; however, their work had much sensitivity and beauty and intensity of feeling that came out of their lives. The poets had a broad range of life experiences. Two were serving life sentences for murder, one woman and another man had spent much of their lives on the streets of Los Angeles, and another man had lost his limbs in a violent drug reprisal. None of the poets were ever writers. No one had ever written anything but a letter. Most were very clumsy with a pen, were initially embarrassed about writing and spelling, and had no idea about how to begin to write a poem.

HOW TO WRITE A POEM

A format called "the sense poem" (Hart and Revheim, 1985) was used. This proved effective in guiding the new poets toward imagery and imagination. It also proved to be effective in keeping each participant on track with the writing and with each other. This was initially one of the primary problems of the group. The sense poem construction format of creating a six-line poem line-by-line was effective in keeping the writers' attentions and also involving the whole group in the construction of each others' poems. It allowed the therapist to help each person develop each line and then attend to special instances of expression and affect that might develop.

The following is a reconstruction of the writing and development of a poem called *Shut-In*. It was a rainy, gloomy morning in southern California, with the dark clouds hanging low over the coastal mountains and rain dripping off the trees. The group seemed low. They had not been able to go off unit for two days due to the rain. The therapist proposed a poem theme of what it was like to be locked up. The group came up with *Shut-In* as a title for a poem. The following line-by-line construction format was used:

- First line—What is the color of Shut-In?
- Second line—What does Shut-In taste like?
- Third line—What does it sound like?
- Fourth line—What does it smell like?
- Fifth line—What does it look like?
- Sixth line—What does it feel like?

Shut-In

by CG

Shut-in is the color blue
and tastes like dry oatmeal.
It sounds like a guitar with no strings
and smells old and musty.
It looks like you're a prisoner
and makes you feel like you are trapped in one room.

Shut-In

by JC

Shut-in is all yellow light
and tastes like weak tea
and smells like an old hospital.
It looks like a locked-up building
and make you feel a lonely sadness.

For each line, each participant was worked with individually, going around the table. Although the format was simple, it was interesting how evocative and different each poem became. Each poet projected his or her own experience and imagery into the same subject. Often this brought responses and discussions from the other group members, which deepened the other group members' own experiences and provoked conversation, sharing, and emotions.

Another theme and title, *Misfortune,* was proposed, and poems were developed using the same six-line construction format:

Misfortune

by RS

Misfortune is gray
it tastes like bitter wine.
It is the sound of dog chewing on a bone.
Misfortune smells like rotten apples
looks like a stormy night
and makes you feel sad and cold.

Misfortune

by JC

Misfortune is pink
it tastes like bitter coffee
sounds like a funeral
smells like cold Mexican food.
It looks like a pretty wall covered with graffiti
and it makes you feel rotten inside.

The sense poem format was augmented by poetry readings by the therapist. The new poets heard different styles of poetry each week, from Pablo Neruda, to Langston Hughes, to Rilke, to Native American poetry. An effort was made to bring in African-American, Mexican, and South American writers and to hear poems in Spanish. The therapist also introduced different kinds of emotions, imageries, and themes of writing.

SPECIAL PROJECTS

As the year progressed and a body of work was assembled, the poets' works were gathered into a book and included in an anthology. These works were displayed during special hospital events and open houses for visitors. A video film record of selected poems was created by the poets and the hospital video department. The poets were proud and pleased at the various displays of their works, and the recognition received seemed to positively affect their self-esteem and pride in their creativity.

CONCLUSIONS AND RECOMMENDATIONS

A search of a wide range of journals from various disciplines, including gerontology, nursing, psychology abstracts, and social work, indicates a proliferation of uses of poetry in practice. This is seen as a reflection of the revival of poetry and the spoken word. It can also be seen as an opportunity for revival of traditional group-work practice methods, theories, and values.

Group work with literature and writing has a long and important tradition in social work. The early settlement-house group workers emphasized the use of activity-oriented group interventions. They emphasized the use of various literary and artistic activities as methods to enhance social functioning and to bring some beauty into the desperately deprived neighborhoods of the settlements. Folk dancing groups, reading groups, drama groups, folk art, and art groups were common formats for group experiences and group education. The learning of cooperative social relations was a key objective (Coyle, 1948).

As Coyle (1948) and others have lamented, the casework influence with its attendant prestige soon overshadowed traditional group work methods. The arts and crafts methods were soon thought to be trivial, simplistic, and beneath the dignity of "professionals" concerned with the dynamic intellectual exploration of intrapsychic forces. The intrapsychic study of the individual became the glamour treatment of choice. This resulted in a gradual but steady move away from the theories, methods, and values of the leaders of social group work such as Neva Boyd, Grace Coyle, Gertrude Wilson, and Gladys Ryland. The gap widened between the socialization and interpersonal development camp and the casework and intrapsychic analytic camp.

This chapter presents a model that is an effort to bridge that gap. Using Howard Gardners' (1983) work on the theory of multiple intelligences as a theory base, and Personality Fitness Training (Hart, 1985) as a working model, a direct link is created to the works of William James and John Dewey, educators, and of Neva Boyd, Grace Coyle, and the other early social group workers.

Lauer (1994) cautions against the abuse of poetry therapy. The most evident abuses are practitioner zeal and indiscriminate applications by incompetent therapists. It is clearly important that the professional group worker follow professional guidelines and exercise good judgment in participant selection, and in management and direction of the group. The therapist assumes several roles in directing this group including teacher, poet, coach, and therapist. Reinsdorf (1994), in an article discussing schizophrenia, poetic imagery, and metaphor, stated that "imagistic poetry attempts to fuse word and thing to present them to our senses for understanding." He believes that the poetic metaphors can help us understand reality. In his comparison of poetic metaphor and schizoid concretism he shows how one succeeds and the other fails in creative imaging.

While there certainly was evidence of concretism in the works of this group of diagnosed long-term schizophrenics, there was also an observed progression in their abilities to create poetic imagism.

Poetry is a powerful, evocative medium for relationships, therapy, catharsis, and understanding. We should use it with tender care, mindful to stay awake while we do so.

A Ritual to Read to Each Other
by William Stafford (1993)

If you don't know the kind of person I am
and I don't know the kind of person you are
a pattern that others made may prevail in the world
and following the wrong god home we may miss our star.

For there is many a small betrayal in the mind,
a shrug that lets the fragile sequence break
sending with shouts the horrible errors of childhood
storming out to play through the broken dike.

And as elephants parade holding each elephant's tail,
but if one wanders the circus won't find the park,
I call it cruel and maybe the root of all cruelty
to know what occurs but not recognize the fact.

And so I appeal to a voice, to something shadowy,
a remote important region in all who talk:
though we could fool each other, we should consider–
lest the parade of our mutual life get lost in the dark.

For it is important that awake people be awake,
or a breaking line may discourage them back to sleep;
the signals we give–yes or no, or maybe–
should be clear: the darkness around us is deep.

BIBLIOGRAPHY

Bly, R. (1990). *American poetry: Wilderness and domesticity.* New York: Harper & Row, pp. 7-35.

Coyle, G. L. (1948). *Group work with American youth.* New York: Harper & Bros.

Doreski, C.K., and Doreski, W. (1988). *How to read and interpret poetry.* New York: Arco, pp. 1-10.

Gardner, H. (1983). *Frames of mind: The theory of multiple intelligences.* New York: Basic Books.

Hart, J. (1985). *Personality fitness training for children and youth: An investigation into the effect of psychological exercise upon self-esteem, stress and school grades.* Unpublished doctoral dissertation, University of Southern California.

Hart, J.L., and Revheim, R. (1985). *Personality fitness training for children and youth.* (Available from J.L. Hart, Alabama A&M University.)

Lauer, R. (1994). Abuses of poetry therapy. In A. Lerner (Ed.), *Poetry in the Therapeutic Experience*. St. Louis: MMB Inc., pp. 73-80.

Magee, J. (1994). Using poetic paradox to enhance the self-esteem of shame driven older adults. *Activities, Adaptation and Aging, 19*:27-35.

Reinsdorf, W. (1994). Schizophrenia, poetic imagery and metaphor. *Imagination, Cognition, and Personality, 13*:335-345.

Reiter, S. (1994). Enhancing the quality of life for the frail elderly: ℞ the poetic prescription. *Journal of Long Term Home Health Care, 13*:12-19.

Simon, P. (Ed.) (1971). *Play and game theory in group work: A collection of the papers of Neva Lona Boyd*. University of Illinois, Jane Addams School of Social Work.

Stafford, W. (1993). A ritual to read to each other. In R. Bly (Ed.), *The darkness around us is deep: Selected poems of William Stafford*. New York: Harper, pp. 135-136

Chapter 13

Refiguring Group-Work Services with People with AIDS

George S. Getzel

Ivan Illich (1982) warned that advanced societies use medical technologies with excessive zeal in an effort to eradicate all unacceptable conditions–physical, social, and moral. Medical technology, in turn, introduces unforeseen diseases and side effects in the human organism, society, and culture. He called the infatuation with this type of solution "medicalization." The individual succumbs to medical definitions and the processes of the health care system that are endowed with *a priori* goodness and magical powers to curb death itself. The AIDS pandemic gives ample testimony to the medicalization of a disease entity with fearsome symptoms and accompanying stigma. Alternatively, groups provide for the "normalization" of the disease sequence and allow members to experience feelings of wellness after diagnosis.

The effectiveness of support groups for persons with AIDS (PWAs) is widely acknowledged (Getzel, 1994). Beginning in community-based organizations, support groups served as an instrument to abet coping with illness and incapacitation. Groups provided a much needed outlet to discuss questions surrounding death and dying. Life-threatening disease creates the potential for morbid preoccupation with illness and its treatment.

This chapter describes a short-term model called the Orientation Support Group for recently diagnosed PWAs trying to live as fully as possible after diagnosis. The Orientation Support Group model allows group members to explore the realistic consequences of the diagnosis and to enter a new world that is not wholly defined by AIDS.

REVIEW OF THE LITERATURE

From the start of the first AIDS service organizations, support groups were recognized as important normalizing experiences for PWAs and their care giving kin and friends (Lopez and Getzel, 1984). The literature, although not large, does point to the widespread use of support groups for special populations in a variety of contexts. Group work models for gay men in community-based organizations are described in some detail (Gambe and Getzel, 1989; Gambe, 1991; Getzel and Mahony, 1989; Getzel, 1991 a,b; Getzel, 1994).

Child and Getzel (1989) described a support group model for poor people in an urban hospital setting, which was crisis-oriented and capable of serving hospitalized and recently released patients with AIDS, including persons with drug histories, women, and gay men of color. PWAs who are intravenous drug users can benefit from group support programs that emphasize "harm reduction strategies" to curtail the use of drugs, while providing social support and guidance about the disease process (Bataki, 1990; O'Dowd et al., 1991). Recently, increased attention has been given to PWAs living in rural areas who are limited in their abilities to attend support groups in distant community-based organizations. Telephone support group-work models have been developed for both PWAs and caregivers to break down the isolation of PWAs in rural areas, but also to protect their anonymity (Rounds et al., 1991). Telephone support groups have also been used for parents who have children with pediatric AIDS (Weiner et al., 1993) and for PWAs who are disabled in the terminal phase of the disease process (Rittner and Hammons, 1992).

Gambe and Getzel (1989) emphasized that groups provide substitutes for weakened or absent social supports in PWAs' lives. Getzel and Mahony (1990) identified the themes of loss and human mortality occurring in the supportive environment of the group.

CLASH OF IDEOLOGIES

The Orientation Support Group approach developed out of concerns about the limits of long-term support groups for PWAs at the

Gay Men's Health Crisis (GMHC) in New York City, the oldest and largest voluntary AIDS service organization in the world. As early as 1982, GMHC encouraged PWAs and care partners to join groups led by mental health professionals who served as volunteers. The ideology of the groups varied from group psychotherapy to group support/self-help. Underlying these differences in clinical ideology were important yet submerged differences among clinicians about the nature of AIDS as a biopsychosocial entity.

Group leaders identified as group psychotherapists tended to define AIDS as a condition associated with stress, dysfunctional mental symptoms, and regression. The group psychotherapist selected "patients" from the waiting list by excluding PWAs on the basis of behavioral and personality attributes judged to be incompatible with group membership. An applicant was unsuitable if clinicians perceived "too much denial" of the disease in a PWA's day-to-day functioning. Rejection was also related to PWAs' behaviors judged to be too flamboyant, histrionic, or self-centered. The psychotherapists valued group stability and demanded that each group member make a long-term commitment to the group.

The clinicians using the support/mutual aid group model took on facilitative roles that encouraged mutual support and self-help inside and outside of the group. Their approach was highly consonant with social-work practice with groups. These group workers encouraged members' exchanges of cognitive guidance, emotional expression, social interaction, instrumental assistance, and material resources in the group and in the wider social environment. Gambe and Getzel (1989) detailed the essential elements of this approach with gay men with AIDS; they identified this as a long-term service model that ended with members' hospitalizations or deaths.

DESIGN CHANGES IN THE 1990s

With the changing character of the AIDS pandemic in New York City and other urban epicenters of the disease, professionals in community-based organizations and others began to question the ubiquitous application of long-term group service approaches to PWAs. In addition, the use of group psychotherapy for PWAs, who were not ostensibly coming for mental health services, became a source of contention for consumers, AIDS advocates, and others. Some very interesting questions arose: How would group services for PWAs with histories of mental illnesses differ from services for PWAs without histories of psychiatric illnesses, or differ for PWAs with the presence of HIV-related dementia? Do the normative stress reactions to AIDS automatically necessitate psychotherapy? Does a differential diagnosis require different group approaches (King, 1993)?

GMHC's clinical staff decided that services should be differentiated to reflect the range of reasons PWAs are seeking groups. The agency had to be more democratic and efficient in its acceptance of clients wanting groups immediately after intake. High selectivity of members for groups and waiting lists were no longer acceptable. In addition, PWAs were no longer dying in great numbers within months of diagnosis from opportunistic infections as was the case in the 1980s.

PWAs, diagnosed but asymptomatic, raised serious concerns about being in groups when other members were becoming very ill and dying. In addition, there was recognition of the large numbers of PWAs living with a diagnosis for five or more years; they had special problems that were not adequately addressed in long-term groups. This significant shift of perceptions in the agency resulted in experimentation with short- as well as long-term groups, and in the offering of groups that focused on the normative difficulties of PWAs at different stages of the disease sequence.

A COMPREHENSIVE GROUP PROGRAM

Currently, GMHC is undergoing a retooling of all its group services. What was once a long-term group-work service for PWAs is a series of specialized groups that reflect with more precision the disease sequence and medical treatment advances. The management of different aspects of everyday life becomes important in groups. For example, women with children must plan for the custody of their children. All persons must consider how they will manage income and health care now and if they later become unemployed or disabled. Cognitive guidance about available health and social services and how to use them becomes an important aspect of group activities. Depression, guilt, shame, and powerlessness are lifted as group members gain understanding about the similarity of their reactions and better coping strategies.

Group homogeneity is an important consideration in the design of an Orientation Support Group. Gay men, male or female intravenous drug users, and women infected by men benefit from homogeneous group composition that allows for more in-depth coverage of shared concerns.

After the completion of the Orientation Support Group, time-limited groups are offered on relationship issues with couples, parents, and siblings, and include bereavement assistance. The assumption of relationship groups is that all close relationships change with serious illness. A group can strategically help with some of these problems: care giving and receiving concerns, breakdowns in communications, domestic conflicts, and intimacy issues.

Finally, Quality of Life Support Groups are offered during periods of serious illness and the end stage of the disease process. Quality of Life Support Groups may not address PWAs' needs until a couple of years after diagnosis. Serious, life-threatening diseases tend to come later.

Particular symptoms of opportunistic disease may warrant special efforts at group composition that allow for homogeneity of membership. A group may be composed of PWAs with visual impairments resulting from cytomegaloviral infections or of PWAs with disfiguring Kaposi's sarcoma lesions. In these groups, the membership can provide empathetic support and the exchange of useful information about resources, such as how to obtain at-home mobility training or cosmetics to disguise facial lesions.

ORIENTATION SUPPORT GROUP AS LINCHPIN

The Orientation Support Group plays an important role in preparing PWAs for living with AIDS and utilizing other group services in the agency. It introduces the themes that are deeper in other groups available to individuals at different points of crisis.

This group's primary focus is assisting members to cope with self-recognition as a person with AIDS. This may also mean coming out of the closet to others as a gay man or as a person with a history of drug abuse.

The group meets for eight consecutive sessions, then participants can choose to join other GMHC-sponsored groups. The group worker helps members make service plans after the Orientation Support Group ends. The topics of the eight sessions occur in this order:

- Introducing each other and starting up (one week)
- Dealing with health and social service providers (one week)
- Family concerns (two weeks)
- Sexuality and intimacy issues (one week)
- Managing serious illness and quality of life concerns (two weeks)
- Transitions and living with AIDS (one week)

Content and Activities

Each session builds on the previous session, moving from system-related problems to family concerns and, finally, to self-related concerns. The emphasis is on making the group a safe and supportive environment, where group members can self-reveal and problem-solve in their own ways and at their own paces. Group sessions begin with an open discussion period, followed by a gentle reprise of the previous session. Video excerpts of a PWA discussing the topical concern of the session are used to stimulate discussion and activities. Group sessions are activity-focused. The activities in the group may include the following: members introducing themselves in terms *unrelated* to AIDS; doing maps of their support systems; role playing conversations with friends who are too quick to reassure; and filling out advanced directive statements that allow kin or friends to make medical decisions.

Case Illustration

The design and format of group sessions are illustrated by excerpts from the sixth session of the Orientation Support Group, which focuses on self-concerns about serious illness, dying, and death. This session uses techniques learned in earlier sessions (video trigger material, group discussion, activities, rehearsal and role-playing).

Sixth Session Excerpts

In the sixth session, group members are introduced to the subject of "quality of life" concerns by seeing a brief video in which a PWA voices concerns about becoming seriously ill and disfigured from disease. He speaks about voluntary active euthanasia and refers to his lack of belief in an afterlife. The PWA discusses his will and advanced directives, going so far as expressing a wish for his cremated remains to be spread in Central Park.

The group worker engages members in a discussion about their reactions to the video. The group members have an animated discussion, quickly making references to themselves. The group worker supports members presenting different points of view. She notes similar and conflicting perspectives shared by members, including a strong need to deny thoughts of death and dying in order to survive day-by-day, contrasting beliefs in an afterlife, revelations of having suicidal thoughts, lack of loved ones' acceptance of their eventual deaths, expressions of dread about painful deaths, and being upset over how survivors will handle their deaths. While some members interact, others are decidedly quiet, still others glassy-eyed.

The group worker summarizes their range of reactions and acknowledges this is a tough subject to address, even at this late date in the life of the group. She asks members to fill out 3×5 cards with pencils supplied. She requests that they not put their names on the cards and write three or more fears they have about becoming seriously ill or dying from AIDS. On the other side of the card, she asks them to write three things that they could do positively to deal with their fears and concerns. Cards are shuffled and distributed to members. They first read aloud fears and concerns and then positive actions, which a group member lists on a flipchart.

The first list has the following: panic attacks about dying, feeling hopeless, suicidal wishes and plans, fears of severe pain, fear of dying alone, frustration that no one wants to hear about dying, fear of becoming impoverished, fear of disfigurement and becoming disabled. . . . As members read this list, there are expressions of agreement and cross-conversations. The second list of positive actions includes the following: reaching out to friends when panicked; seeking psychiatric help; talking to a trusted friend about suicidal ideas and plans; making advanced directives; talking to your doctor about your treatment wishes in advance; planning your funeral and prepaying for it; talking about death, before others raise it; speaking to your loved ones about your concerns about how they will fare after your death; using prayer, guided imagery, and meditation; and allowing yourself to grieve in advance over your prospective death.

Paradoxically the tone of the meeting seems to lighten as their anonymous fears and concerns are read out loud and listed on a flipchart. Group members become highly animated after positive actions are listed. As the meeting ends, the group worker distributes blank advanced directive forms to members that are to be filled out as best they can before the next session. The group will be discussing advanced directives and wills at their next session. The group worker stays outside the room while some members speak to her privately.

Discussion

The use of the Orientation Support Group opens up a range of more democratically run and consumer-oriented support groups for PWAs and their care givers. Group-work practice must change and become consonant with the changing nature of the AIDS pandemic. As opposed to just giving "support" to PWAs, we must look at what are the appropriate types of support needed by PWAs at different points in their management of day-to-day living.

Group support can be professionally guided or led by trained volunteers and consumers. Consumers often have leadership skills as well as knowledge, which ought to be harnessed as sources of role modeling and support. The Orientation Support Group is specified in detail, which allows for the use of volunteer leaders.

The Orientation Support Group gives the practitioner information for assessing future needs of PWAs. The experience also prepares PWAs to be more knowledgeable consumers.

CONCLUSION

Unfortunately, the AIDS pandemic relentlessly continues. Large numbers of social workers with groups must be enlisted in developing effective outreach services for different populations in need. We must harness the power and healing capacity of groups of PWAs battling valiantly for freedom, hope, and existence.

REFERENCES

Bataki, S.L. (1990). Substance abuse and AIDS: The need for mental health services. *New Directions in Mental Health Services*, 48:55-67.

Child, R. and Getzel, G. S. (1989). Group work with inner city people with AIDS. *Social Work with Groups*, 12(4):65-80.

Gambe, R. (1991). Group therapy with people with AIDS/Kaposi's sarcoma. In M. Weil, K. Chau, and D. Southerland (Eds.), *Theory and practice of social group work: Creative solutions*. Binghamton, NY: The Haworth Press, Inc., pp. 107-120.

Gambe, R. and Getzel, G.S. (1989). Group work with gay men with AIDS. *Social Casework*, 70(3):172-179.

Getzel, G.S. (1991a). AIDS. In A. Gitterman (Ed.), *Handbook of social work with vulnerable populations*. New York: Columbia, pp. 35-64.

Getzel, G.S. (1991b). Survival modes of people with AIDS in groups. *Social Work*, 36(1):7-11.

Getzel, G.S. (1994) No one is alone: Groups during the AIDS pandemic. In A. Gitterman and L. Shulman (Eds.), *Mutual aid groups, vulnerable populations, and the life cycle*. New York: Columbia, pp. 185-197.

Getzel, G.S. and Mahony, K. (1990). Confronting human finitude: Group work with people with AIDS. *Journal of Gay and Lesbian Psychotherapy*, 1(3):105-120.

Illich, I. (1982). *The medical nemesis: The expropriation of health*. New York: Pantheon.

King, M.B. (1993). *AIDS, HIV and mental health*. UK: Cambridge.

Lopez, D.J. and Getzel, G.S. (1984). Helping gay patients in crisis. *Social Casework*, 65:387-394.

O'Dowd, M.A., Natalie, C., Orr, D., and McKegney, F. (1991). Characteristics of patients attending an HIV-related psychiatric outpatient clinic. *Hospital and Community Psychiatry*, 42(6):615-619.

Rittner, B., and Hammons, K. (1992). Telephone group work with people with end stage AIDS. *Social Work with Groups*, 15(4):59-72.

Rounds, K.A., Galinsky, M.J., and Stevens, L.S. (1991). Linking people with AIDS in rural communities: The telephone group. *Social Work*, 36(1):13-18.

Weiner, L.S., Spencer, E.D., Davidson, R., and Fair, C. (1993). National telephone support groups: A new avenue toward psychosocial support for HIV-infected children and their families. *Social Work with Groups*, 16(3):55-71.

Chapter 14

Post-Transplant Group . . . Five Years On

Joanne Avery

INTRODUCTION

I will begin by describing the history of the group, how and why it started, and define the type. The roles of facilitator and social work student will be described, as well as the nature of the group itself, and its membership and format. Methods of support that are integral to the group will be discussed and themes identified, with examples. Group-work skills will be considered, and the "Buddy system," unique to this group, will be described in detail. Questions about the nature of boundaries, possible preventative aspects, and member need satisfaction will also be addressed.

BACKGROUND

I would first like to offer some background information about Autologous Bone Marrow Transplant or ABMT. This treatment involves giving large doses of intravenous chemotherapy drugs to eliminate the disease, followed by the restoration of the patient's bone marrow. In the Toronto Hospital ABMT program, patients' own bone marrows and/or blood stem cells are "harvested," frozen, then retransfused after the patients receive potentially lethal doses of chemotherapy, and possibly radiation treatment, for their cancers. The average length of stay is four to six weeks including a period of isolation (15 to 30 days).

HISTORY

In 1989, three years after the ABMT program began, a pilot project was initiated under my direction, to develop a list of former patients, now "survivors," who would be willing to become "Buddies" for new patients. This concept was generated initially by one of our early ABMT patients (Dan) who persisted in lobbying me until I was able to develop a plan for implementation.

I assigned my social work student, Viviane, to gather support across all health care disciplines. Once accomplished, she invited 16 selected "survivors" to an information meeting in fall of 1990. Of these 16 "survivors," 6 came to the first meeting. From this small focus group of six enthusiastic individuals sprang the concept of a peer support group whose focus would be twofold:

1. To offer a Buddy system for new patients requesting help pre-transplant
2. To provide support for each other, both in the roles of Buddies and as fellow "survivors"

As noted by Cella and Yellen (1993), an important ingredient of any cancer support group is the identification of the universality of member experience and identity. Although some of these individuals had been hospitalized in adjacent rooms, they had not met before. Interpersonal alienation existed despite the efforts of their supportive families and health care team.

A group would provide a safe forum to discuss information and concerns common to everyone while a Buddy system would counter-act this same alienation for new patients who were approaching their transplants.

IMPORTANCE OF GROUP SUPPORT

Stressors specific to all ABMT patients (Herschl, 1992) are the following:

- Experimental nature of treatment
- Disruption in life cycle
- Isolation required for lowered immune system
- Toxic preconditioning required
- Transplantation experience magical/paradoxical
- Physical/pain debilitation

- Protracted waiting period
- Length of recovery (one to two years)

Under "length of recovery," Herschl (1992) described in detail the many factors peculiar to ABMT patients:

- Chronicity of symptoms
- Potential for late physiological effects
- Fear of disease recurrence
- Deficits in functioning
- Diminished physical attractiveness
- Loss of identity/self-esteem
- Effect of illness on family/interpersonal relationships
- Potential loss of employment or job discrimination
- Financial indebtedness

It has been found in several recent quality of life (QOL) studies (Haberman et al., 1993; Wingard et al., 1992; Bush et al., 1995; Chao et al., 1992; Ferrell et al., 1992) that despite these difficulties, given an adequate degree of support, the majority of ABMT survivors are able to regain their pretransplant levels of life satisfaction. Ferrell et al. asked 119 ABMT survivors, "What could physicians or nurses do to improve your QOL?" and identified six themes. The need to provide support groups was emphasized not only for post-ABMT patients but for pretransplant patients as well. The areas of need encompassed were peer support for patients and their families, information, education about symptoms, and increased understanding during the readjustment phase following transplant.

ROLE OF FACILITATOR

Due to the design of the pilot project, the group was chaired and coordinated for the first two years by social work students: Viviane in 1990 and Linda in 1991. Cella and Yellen (1993) have produced a set of beliefs known as the Cancer Wellness Doctrine, which is intended as a framework for conceptualizing responses to interactions within cancer-related groups. The doctrine includes the following value-based goals:

- To promote cohesion; to develop a safe climate; to help support evolve
- To offer generous reinforcement; to foster stress reduction; to give information

In order to achieve cohesion, the facilitator must encourage constructive rather than destructive processes by minimizing distances among group members and between the group and the facilitator, and by using consensus in decision making whenever possible. A safe climate is promoted by helping members to accept one anothers' differences, and protecting them from excessive demands for self-disclosure. Education and empowerment of members helps support develop in the group; rewarding positive, productive behaviors can promote self-esteem.

These directives, although expressed as a theory, reflect the essence of a good support-group facilitator. For example, regarding self-esteem, one member, Russ, was a self-professed "nongroupie." Nevertheless he managed to commit himself to produce the newsletter for the group, and even attended a few meetings including one immediately following the recurrence of his disease. Prior to this meeting, Russ confided that he was worried that his presence might cause others to be upset; however, I encouraged him to attend. At that meeting, Russ described to the other members, in his own unique way, how he was dealing with this new threat to his life. He explained that he had chosen to consider himself as a player in a computer game where there was always another door to enter and another room to explore and conquer. Rather than retreat passively when a further threat loomed, he dared to place himself as an active participant in a game. The room was silent. . . . As the group digested the impact of his words, I worried that they might be so overwhelmed with their own fears of recurrence that they would not be able to respond positively. Instead, the other members supported him enthusiastically in his fight for life, and gathered strength from his example of courage. In this way, the group managed to express their positive feelings and admiration for him. For Russ, the acceptance of the group meant that he was not alone, that others could relate to what he was experiencing. At the most recent meeting of the group, more than two years later, one of the members spoke again of Russ's generosity and how his strong presence in the group had impressed her.

It is only when the members can openly share in the search for knowledge and meaning that it is possible to learn what each member can offer. I have learned there are many talents that people possess that would not otherwise be accessible. I tend to be impatient at times, and want to hurry the discussion along. On occasion as I have been "chewing at the bit," I have been rewarded with a wonderful insight or different perspective that would not otherwise have emerged if I had simply followed my own agenda.

The role of facilitator has altered over the past five years to accommodate the growth and gradual emergence of leadership from within the group. In the beginning, I felt it was necessary to stimulate the formation of the group by planning the agenda, telephoning the members to ensure attendance, and providing refreshments. Gradually, I have been able to draw back and allow the membership to assume increased responsibilities for coordination and planning.

NATURE OF GROUP SUPPORT

In the ABMT peer support group, our objectives are simple: to provide encouragement to other members, to share information, to help members cope, to respect members' individuality—to help each individual find personal meaning and a sense of belonging by participating in the group process.

The Buddy system is modeled after the Toronto Hospital Renal Peer Support program and consists of one-to-one emotional support offered pre/during/after ABMT. In order to become a Buddy, an individual must be posttransplant for one and a half to two years and be considered suitable by the transplant team. Matching of Buddies and patients is managed through the social worker so that careful attention is paid to the many factors involved. Matching variables include illness, age, sex, type of treatment, personality, developmental stage, and location.

A Buddy request is initiated via flyers posted in the clinic, ABMT Information Booklet, or directly to the social worker. The patient is then contacted by the social worker and relevant information is gathered. The social worker then contacts the appropriate buddy and requests his or her assistance. In this way, the buddy is able to learn a little about the patient and decide if he or she is able to provide the service, prior to being in touch with the patient.

Contact can begin immediately after exchange of information has taken place and usually involves weekly telephone contact and occasional visits in person. Since ABMT can take as long as six months or more, contact ranges from a few months to well over a year. The emotional and spiritual impact of meeting someone who has undergone the transplant and survived cannot be underestimated! In the words of one of our buddies,

> At the time of my transplant I asked for help, for a Buddy, from the Reach to Recovery program, and was told that because it was Christmas, there was no one available to help me. I never *had* a Buddy! I believe that this was a major factor in determining that Tony (my husband) and I didn't hesitate for one minute when we were first asked if we would talk to another lady who was contemplating this radical treatment. We were determined that if *we* could help it, no one else would be left alone like I was. Being a Buddy lets us be positive and caring, and it helps our helpers to give other cancer victims as good a fighting chance as they've given us. That seems important.

MEMBERSHIP AND FORMAT

Criteria for group membership has been determined by the steering committee to include both pre- and posttransplant patients. Even though the original purpose for the group was to provide Buddies, not all members were ready to take on this role. The steering committee has acknowledged this fact and incorporated those needs for posttransplant support into the philosophy of the group.

The meetings are held at the hospital every six weeks for three hours with 15 to 30 members attending. Topics have included the following:

- Mother's account of 19-year-old son's death
- Recurrence rate
- Use of immune stimulator drugs
- Gene marking studies

Future topics under consideration include the following:

- Fertility/infertility–patients' experiences with artificial insemination
- Liver complications posttransplant (Hepatitis C)
- Role changes after ABMT

Following the death of one of our group members, it was decided to introduce a ritual–the lighting of a candle–at the beginnings of our meetings, to remember those who have died. Members form a circle and the meeting generally starts with a "go-around" during which members share brief accounts of their current activities, their diagnoses, as well as reports on their Buddy work at present. The topic for the evening is introduced by the chair and a discussion is held. It is customary to have a break part way through the evening and at this time, much informal but important networking takes place.

SUPPORTIVE ELEMENTS AND THEMES

Chao et al. (1992) has identified five elements of support that are usually present in groups of this type: maintenance of social identity, provision of emotional support, tangible environmental support, information, and social affiliation.

The preferred identities of the group members as "graduates" rather than survivors represents their firm decisions to view their transplants definitely as part of the past and as something that has been "achieved" or "earned." Members have consciously rejected the term "survivor" as a concept in the same category as the term "victim."

Emotional support is offered at all points throughout the group, such as during the initial sharing of memories about a member who has died (the candle ritual), to discussion of a problem common to all (e.g., feelings about hair loss due to the treatment), to simply receiving the Peer Support newsletter (a general sharing of information and update about members). The tone of the meetings moves from "chatty" to "intimate," with genuine emotions being expressed by all attending.

Information sharing is a regular part of group meetings through announcements, discussions, presentations, and the U.S. ABMT

Newsletter. This is a vital need and an ongoing function of the group, since new treatments and protocols are constantly being developed and members have expressed strong desires to keep informed–not only for themselves but also their Buddies.

Certain themes are common to the group:

> *Intrapsychic:* loss of health or Buddies; fears of dying or recurrence; new treatments or complications; anger about physical changes; pain; and denial
> *Interpersonal:* toll on marital relationships and/or families and/or friends; dependency on others; infertility; role adjustments; changes in relationships
> *Social:* return to work; stigma of cancer; enforced isolation due to medical conditions
> *Cancer:* the transplant itself and its financial costs

ELEMENTS IMPORTANT TO STAFF/GROUP RELATIONSHIP

Hope

The most important element is the tangible message of hope, which the physical presence of the members instills, not only for each other and new patients (their Buddies), but just as importantly for staff. For example, a pretransplant patient attending for the first time reported that seeing and hearing the others speak strongly encouraged him.

I recently met a former ABMT nurse who asked me about one of our patients. I replied that she was fine, had married, and was enjoying a "normal" life. A look of amazement spread over her face as she realized that something, which she had not even dared to hope, was indeed true.

Information

Information, such an important tool in coping with illness, is exchanged readily between group members and staff. It is often from the members that I learn of the most recent trends in treatment, whether alternative or traditional. Their thirst for knowledge is insatiable, and even after six to seven years post ABMT, graduates eagerly seek out facts about new methods of treating their illness.

Peer Support

It is also rewarding to witness the power of peer support. An ABMT graduate had completed his initial recovery but was unsure about returning to his former employment. He wondered if it would be too difficult for him to manage, if he would fit in, and if he really wanted to return to that occupation. The other members provided the most effective direction, and offered encouragement for him to try again.

Bonding

There is a sense of bonding and catharsis that may occur at the beginnings and heighten towards the closes of group meetings. It seems to happen in conjunction with discussion around a sensitive topic or a moment of shared laughter. I feel it is indicative of the depth of trust and safety that the group is capable of generating.

Boundaries

There is a shift in boundaries that occurs after patients enter the phase of life known as survivorship following their ABMTs. There is so little known about this time of adjustment, that the distance between staff and patients seems to shrink. Survivors become the experts and staff must look to them to gather knowledge about this aspect of their recoveries.

PREVENTATIVE ASPECTS

As of 1995, from a total of 450 ABMTs performed, over 80 Buddy matches have been accomplished. This figure demonstrates the determination of graduates to provide help to those who have followed them; to ease their anxieties, allow free access to ask those questions they were afraid to bother the doctor with, and provide role models for coping.

The group also offers the opportunity for members to take on different roles that they might not otherwise attempt. In a supportive atmosphere, members can try out new behaviors that are conducive to empowerment and self-esteem. The benefits have proven to be an increased sense of worth, a sense of purpose, and increased abilities in communication and collaboration.

CHALLENGES

There are many challenges that remain to be overcome. Training of Buddies must become a yearly event as the number of Buddy requests continue to put pressure on the number of Buddies available. Particularly in the recent illnesses being treated with ABMT, e.g., breast cancer and multiple myeloma, our limited resources are being heavily utilized. If we are to avoid burnout for our volunteers, it is important not to overload them with too many Buddy referrals.

The number and variety of treatment protocols continues to grow and knowledge of them is required to service those patients involved. This is a responsibility for both the social worker and the Buddy.

Adequate supervision of Buddies is not available since there is only one social worker for the entire patient population.

Evaluation is needed to understand more accurately how new patients are benefitting from their Buddies' contacts and supports. In contrast, we also need to know how this involvement has helped the Buddy himself/herself.

I do know that the atmosphere in our clinics has transformed over the past few years. The tone has changed from a tense, quiet place where people whispered, to one where people gather in small groups and chat openly about their progresses or recent problems. Since one particularly friendly graduate was diagnosed with a recurrence of lymphoma, a special gathering has developed in the clinic of similarly affected patients, where information and support are exchanged without hesitation. Although this person has not returned to the support group, he and his wife have become central to this informal clinic group. Some of these patients remain in contact socially and provide much needed emotional support even up until the point of a member's death. This indicates an increased level of trust and sharing, not only between patients in the clinic, but also the medical staff who accept this need to relate to one another.

Other nonABMT patients have also been affected by this relaxed atmosphere in the clinic. They too are beginning to reach out to others like themselves and are offering to help each other with their goals. As one patient (Carmela) phrased it, after donating the proceeds from her donor campaign to a seriously ill patient, "Even if I can't be helped, then at least someone else still can." It is precisely this atmosphere of generosity that permeates the ABMT peer support group to create the rich environment needed for full rehabilitation of its members.

BIBLIOGRAPHY

Bush N, Haberman M, Donaldson G, and Sullivan K. (1995). Quality of life of 125 adults surviving 6-18 years after bone marrow transplantation. *Social Science Medicine*, 40(4):479-490.

Cella DF, and Yellen S. (1993). Cancer support groups, the state of the art. *Cancer Practice*, May/June: 56-61.

Chao N, Tierney K, Bloom J, Long G, Barr T, Stallbaum B, Wong R, Negrin R, Horning S, and Blume D. (1992). Dynamic assessment of quality of life after autologous bone marrow transplantation. *Blood*, 80(3):825-830.

Ferrell B, Grant M, Schmidt G, Rhiner M, Whitehead C, Fonbuena P, and Forman S. (1992a). The meaning of quality of life for bone marrow transplant survivors. Part I. *Cancer Nursing*, 15(3):153-160.

Ferrell B, Grant M, Schmidt G, Rhiner M, Whitehead C, Fonbuena P, and Forman S. (1992b). The meaning of quality of life for bone marrow transplant survivors. Part II. *Cancer Nursing*, 15(4):247-253.

Futterman A, Wellisch D, Bond G, and Carr C. (1991). The psychosocial levels system. *Psychosomatics*, 32(2) Spring:177-186.

Haberman M, Bush N, Young K, and Sullivan K. (1993). Quality of life of adult long-term survivors of bone marrow transplantation: A qualitative analysis of narrative data. *Oncology Nursing Forum*, 20(10):1545-1553.

Herschl J. (1992). Quality of life: A redefinition of life after bone marrow transplantation. NAOSW Eighth Annual Conference. Unpublished paper.

Mailick M. (1979). The impact of severe illness on the individual and family: An overview. *Social Work in Health Care*, 5(2) Winter:101-113.

Pot-Mees C, and Zeitlin H. (1987). Psychosocial consequences of bone marrow transplantation in children: A preliminary communication. *Journal of Psychosocial Oncology*, 5(2) Summer:73-81.

Wingard J, Curbow B, Baker F, and Piantadosi S. (1991). Health, functional status, and employment of adult survivors of bone marrow transplantation. *Annals of Internal Medicine*, 114:113-118.

Index

A priori goodness, 151

AASWG. *See* Association for the Advancement of Social Work with Groups

ABMT. *See* Autologous Bone Marrow Transplant

Acceptance by peers, 111

Accommodating, 66

Activities of committees, 42-43

Activity groups, 39

Adams, D., 51

Addiction, 51

Administrative committees, 41-42

Administrative groups, 37-38

Affirming conflict, 73

Aggressive behavior, 110

Aging, 33-36

Aging and Mental Health, 33

AIDS pandemic, 151
  changes in, 153-154

Alissi, A., 89

Alumnae Empowerment group, 25

Ambivalence, worker, 62-63

Analysis technique, 83

Anderson, J., 125

Andragogic teaching methods, 50

Andrews, J., 47,48

Anger toward leader, 69-70

Antagonism, 68

Approach, empowerment group, 17-18,24

Art projects, 105

Aspects of prevention, 169-170

Assertiveness, 64

Association for the Advancement of Social Work with Groups, 7,127
  Symposia, 10

Atmosphere, in clinics, 170

Auerbach, C., 126

Autologous Bone Marrow Transplant, 161
  graduate, 169
  history of, 161-162
  information booklet, 165
  length of recovery, 163
  newsletter, 167-168
  non patient, 171
  nurse, 168
  peer support group, 165
  stressors to patients, 162-163
  survivors, 163

Avoiding, 67

Awareness, 72

Bandura, A., 105

Battered women, 17

Beaumont, J., 25

Behavioral approach, 112

Bell, N., 92

"The Bells," 135

Berman-Rossi, T., 9,23

"Billy," 136-137

Birnbaum, M., 126

Blaming, 19

Bly, R. (poet), 144

Board Health Services Committee, 43

Bond, J., 66

Bonding, 169

Boundaries, 169

Bourdon, G., 28

Boyd, N., 148

Brenda (member of
     an empowerment group)
     27-29
Breton, M., 5,22
Brown, A., 10
Buddy match, 169
Buddy request, 165,170
Buddy system, 161,165
Bullying in groups, 89-99
Burnell, G., 48
Burnside, I., 34
Butler, R., 33,35,41

Calm, 72
Cancer (group theme), 168
Cancer Wellness Doctrine, 163-164
Capitulation, 127
Cella, D., 162,163
Challenge, 170-171
"Changed Heart," 137-138
Chao, N., 167
Chaos, 8
Charybdis, 140
Child, R., 152
Children with emotional disability,
     109-111
     and social interaction, 111-112
     transition into public school, 115
Clinic, atmosphere of, 170
Coding, 83
Cofacilitators, 134,140
Cognitive guidance, 154
Cohen, M., 9
Cohesiveness, 104,164
Collaborating, 66
Commission on Group Work
     Education, 127
Committee activities/functions,
     42-43
Committee on Aging, 37
Commonality of social-work
     practice, 125
Communication
     expressed, 62

Communication (continued)
     monitoring, 73-74
     and workers' roles, 23-24
Community, 22
     Building, 138-139
     interventions, 98-99
Competing, 66
Complaint, 67
     discouragement of, 98
Concentration curriculum, 126
Conflict, 61-62
     affirming, 73
     and assertiveness, 64
     positive effects of, 63-65,75
     -response modes, 65-67
     sources of in group, 68-69
Conflict management, strategies,
     70-75
Confrontation, 74
Conscientization, 17
     and critical education, 24
Consciousness raising, 11
Constructivism, 1-4,5,11-12
Council on Social Work Education
     policy statement, 123-129
Countant-Sassic, D., 63
Cox, E., 20
Coyle, G., 148
Creative expression, 131
Critical consciousness, 106-107
Critical education,
     and conscientization, 24
CSWE. See Council on Social Work
     Education
Cultural aspects, sensitivity to, 51
Curriculum policy statement, 127
Curriculum Policy Statement
     for Master's Degree
     Programs in Social Work
     Education, 124

Danesh, H., 64
Data display, 83
Davies, N., 2-3
Death of group member, 167

Decision making, 7-10
  and turntaking, 9,12
  by voting, 8
Deficit of social skills, 110,113
Delphi group, 80
Depression, 50
Deviation from norms, 71
Dewey, J., 148
Differences, 72-73
Dimensions of empowerment, 19
Discouraging complaining, 98
Discussion group, 79
Disenchantment, 69
Distribution of regional summaries,
  83
Diversion, 94
Duffy, T., 9

Education, 38
Ego support, 94-97
Elder, J., 10
Elements of support, 167
Emotional disability, children
  with, 109-111
  and social interaction, 111-112
  transition into public school, 115
Emotional support, 167
Empowerment, 29
  dimensions of, 19
Empowerment group, 15-17,21-22
  approach, 17-18,24
Encyclopedia of Social Work, 47
Estes, R., 17
Evaluation, 171
  case study, 52-56
Expressed communication, 62

Facilitator, 140
  role of, 163-165
"Fair play," 111
Family, reconnection with, 103
Feedback, 72
Festinger, L., 64

Focus group, 80-82
  advantage of using, 83
  questions, 56-57
Focusing on relational issues, 72
Format of group, 166-167
Formation of women's group, 25-27
Frank, J., 68
Freire, P., 24
Functions of committees, 42-43

Galinsky, M., 69
Gambe, R., 152
Gardner, H., 148
Garland, J., 93,94,95
Garvin, C., 125
Gay Men's Health Crisis, 153,154
Gender differences, 65-66
"Generalist," 125
"Generic," 125
Geographical selectivity, 3
Germain, C., 20
Gesme, C., 48
Getzel, G., 152
Gitterman, A., 7-8,9,20,22
GMHC. *See* Gay Men's Health
  Crisis
Goal-directed management, 36
Goldberg-Wood, G., 20,23
Granvold, D., 47
Greenwood, E., 123
Groom, J., 110
Group interview, 80
Group membership, 166-167
Group processes, 116-119,127
Group support
  importance of, 162-163
  nature of, 165-166
Group-work education
  inadequate, 126
  obstacles to, 129
Groups, 24-25
  activity, 39
  administrative, 37-38
  and AIDS, 154-155
  bullying in, 89-99

Groups *(continued)*
  and conflict management, 61-62
  focus, 80-82
    advantage of using, 83
  Orientation Support Group, 151
    linchpin of, 155-158
  personal growth, 44
  poetry
    purpose and goals, 134-135
    structure and composition,
      133-134
    writer's workshop, 144
  post-transplant, 161-163
  psychoeducational, 47-57
  and research, 79-87
  scapegoating in, 89-99
  for senior participation, 40-42
  service provision, 43
  and social relationships, 44
  sources of conflict in, 68-69
  system maintenance, 42-43
  support, 38
Groups and empowerment theory,
  15-17,21-22
Guinier, L., 8
Guralnick, M., 110
Gutiérrez, L., 21

Handicapped vs. nonhandicapped,
  110,119
Hansen, J., 69
Harris, F., 18
Health care, scapegoating in, 92
Here-and-now, 71-72
Herschl, J., 163
High Level Wellness Group, 44
High-status peers, 115
Hinds, C., 82
Hirayama, K., 89
History of Autologous Bone Marrow
  Transplant, 161-162
Hocker, J., 62
Homeless men, 101-107
Hope, 168

Hospital, and poetry, 143-144
Huberman, M., 83
Humor, 27
Hunzeker, J., 20

"I" statement, 74
Ideologies, clash of, 152-153
Illich, I., 151
Implementation (case study), 52-56
Improving group practice, 84-87
Inadequate group-work education,
  126
Inadequate preparation, 129
Individuals, 64
Influence of group, 80
Information, 168-169
Information sharing, 167-168
Integration
  of group-work content, 127
  of social-work practice, 125
Interactional processes, 95
Interactionist approach
  and mutual-aid group, 22-23
Interdisciplinary psychoeducational
  programs, 48
Internal leadership, 136-138
Interpersonal (group theme), 168
Interpretation, 2
Interventions (twelve commonly
  used), 93-97
Intrapsychic (group theme), 168

James, W., 148
John Paul II (Pope), 29-30
Joslyn Senior Center, 37

Kilmann, R., 66
Kissman, K., 132
Knowledge, 2
Kolevzon, M., 126
Kolodny, R., 93,94,95
Kuechler, C., 47,48
Kurland, R., 7

Language, 4-5
Lartin, J., 92
laSalvia, T., 48
Lauer, R., 148
Leader, anger toward, 69-70
Leadership, 49-50
   competent, 50
Leighninger, L., 125
Length of recovery, 163
Lewis, E., 22,51
Life on the street, 102
Listening. *See* Communication
Los Angeles County Area Agency
   on Aging, 38

MacKenzie, K., 70
Mahony, K., 152
Mainstream model, 23
Management
   goal-directed, 36
   service-oriented, 36
Mancoske, R., 20
Marley, J., 49
Master's level field placement, 85
Meaning, 2,3
Measurement, 84
Medical technology, 151
Medicalization, 151
Methods skills, 125
Middleman, R., 20,23
Miles, M., 83
Mirroring, 68
"Misfortune," 146
Mistry, T., 10
Monitoring communication, 73-74
Monitoring group practice, 84
Moral selectivity, 3
MSP. *See* My Sisters' Plane
Mt. San Antonio Gardens, 41,42,44
Mullender, A., 23,140-141
Multilogue, 6-7,12
Multiple intelligences, 148
Mutual-aid group, and interactionist
   approach, 22-23

Mutual aid system, 79,141
My Sisters' Place, 24-25

Names, 26
Neugarten, B., 37
Neumann, 91
Newsweek, 5
Newstetter, W., 42
Nicholas, M., 67
Nominal technique, 80
NonABMT patient, 171
Nondefensive, remaining, 74-75
Nonhandicapped vs. handicapped,
   110,119
Norms, establishing, 70-71
Northen, H., 20
"No violence," 71

Obstacles, 129
Others, involvement with, 101-104
Open communication, 98
Oppression
   and social work, 20-21
   subtle, 10-11
Orientation Support Group, 151
   as linchpin, 155-158
Outcomes of group processes,
   116-119

Pain, 144
Papell, C., 23
Paranoid ideation, 67
Parents, 111
Parry, J., 128
Parsons, R., 20
PCs. *See* Penal code patients
Pediatric AIDS, 152
Peer acceptance, 111
Peer rejection, 111,112
Peer support, 169
Penal code patients, 143
Pernell, R., 21
Personal conflict-response modes,
   65-67

Personal enhancement, 38
Personal growth groups, 44
Personal/political power, 18-21
Personality Fitness Training, 148
Persons with AIDS, 151,152,154
Poetry
    and community building, 138-139
    and creative expression, 131-133
    how to write, 145-147
    and the state hospital setting,
        143-144
Political pressure, 129
Post-transplant group, 161-163
Power, 5-6
    personal/political, 18-21
Power of Words, The, 4
Powerless, 19,21,129
Practice
    effective, 51-52
    implications, 6
    responsible, 51-52
Practice-research approach, 87
Preventing scapegoating, 97-99
Prevention, aspects of, 169-170
Problem solving skills, 113
Privacy, 102
Process of group work, 127
Process statement, 74
Professionals' biases, 3
"Projection of the shadow," 91
Propaganda, 3
Protection, 94
Psychoeducational groups, 47-57
Public school, transition into, 115
"Pure" education, 50-52
Purpose, 49
PWAs. *See* Persons with AIDS

QOL. *See* Quality of life studies
Quality of life studies, 163
Quality of Life Support Groups, 155
Questions, focus group, 56-57

Raising consciousness, 11
Reconnection with family, 103
Recreation, 39
Reducing interaction, 94
Reid, K., 69
Reid, W., 125
Reinsdorf, W., 148
Rejection by peers, 111,112
Relational issues, focusing on, 72
Research, and groups, 79-87
Resident organizations, 42
Resolution, 70
Response to curriculum policy
        statement, 127-128
Retirement, 33-36
    communities, 40-41
Rewards, use of, 112
Rilke (poet), 144
"A Ritual to Read Each Other," 149
Rivas, R., 51
Role assigning, 95
Role assuming, 95
Rothman, B., 23
Ryland, G., 148

Saleebey, D., 20
Salmon, R., 7
Sarri, R., 69
Scapegoat, functions of, 91-93
Scapegoating in groups, 89-99
Schizophrenia, 50
Schmidt, M., 34
Schwartz, W., 22,23
Scylla, 140
Selected social work, 128
Self-devaluation, 35
Self-directed task group, 132
    and the worker, 140-141
Self-efficacy, 105-106
Self-esteem, 53,104
Self-Esteem Support Group,
        52,53-54
Senior centers, 35,37
Senior participation groups, 40-41
Sense poem, 145,146

Service-oriented management, 36
Service provision groups, 43-44
Settlement Movement, 99
Sexual alliances, 102
Shapiro, B., 21-22
Sharing, 66
Sheehy, G., 35
Shulman, L., 20,22,90,91,95
"Shut-In," 145-146
Simon, B., 19
Situating practice-research, 85
Skills, 104-105
Skills generalist, 125
Smith, E., 69
Social (group theme), 168
Social interaction, 111-112
Social reality, 3,4
Social relationships, groups for, 44
Social skills deficit, 110,113
Social skills program, 113-116
Social work
    mainstream model of, 23
    and oppression, 20
Social Work, 5-6
Social Work with Groups, 6
Social-work practice, 125
Society, value system, 101
Sociometric measures, 118
Solomon, B., 19
Solution to scapegoating, 95-96
Special school/classroom placement,
    110
Squashing, 93-94
Stafford, W., 149
State Arts Commission, 132
State hospital, and poetry, 143-144
"Staying out," 106,107
Stereotypes, 3
Strachey, J., 71
Strategy, conflict management,
    70-75
Street life, 102
Stressors to Autologous Bone
        Marrow Transplant patients,
        162-163

Structure of poetry group, 134
Subtle oppression, 10-11
Successful women's group, 26,29.
    See also Brenda
Support, elements of, 167
Support groups, 38,153
System maintenance groups, 42-43

Targeting group, 96-97
Targeting the scapegoat, 96
Taylor, P., 48
Theoretical foundations, 48-49
Thomas, K., 66
Time-out room, 112
Tolerance of differences, 98
Tolson, E., 125
Toronto Hospital Renal Peer Support
        program, 165
Toseland, R., 51
Transference, 68
Transformation, 20
    of curriculum policy statement,
        123-127
Transition into public school, 115
Transition into retirement, 38
Triangulation, 87
Tuckman, B., 69
Turntaking, 7-10,103
    and decision making, 9,12

Unseasoned worker, 63

Value system, 101
Victim blaming, 19
Victimization, 15,17
Viewer, 1
Vinacke, W., 66
Violence, 144
    gang, 18
Vogel, E., 92
Voting, and decision making, 8

Wall of barriers, 26
Ward, D., 23,141
Warner, R., 69
Well-functioning group, 69
Wilmot, W., 62
Wilson, G., 148
"Winter Dreaming," 133-134
Women
    battered, 17
    empowerment group, 25-29
Wong, F., 63
Worchel, S., 63
Words from the Curb, 139

Worker
    ambivalence, 62-63
    attack on, 69
    roles, and communication, 23-24
    and self-directed groups, 140-141
Worshipful attitude, 69
Writer's workshop, poetry, 144
Writing a poem, 145-147

Yalom, I., 63,68
Yellen, S., 162,163

Order Your Own Copy of
This Important Book for Your Personal Library!

FROM PREVENTION TO WELLNESS THROUGH GROUP WORK

_____in hardbound at $49.95 (ISBN: 0-7890-0164-0)

COST OF BOOKS_____

OUTSIDE USA/CANADA/
MEXICO: ADD 20%_____

POSTAGE & HANDLING_____
*(US: $3.00 for first book & $1.25
for each additional book)
Outside US: $4.75 for first book
& $1.75 for each additional book)*

SUBTOTAL_____

IN CANADA: ADD 7% GST_____

STATE TAX_____
*(NY, OH & MN residents, please
add appropriate local sales tax)*

FINAL TOTAL_____
*(If paying in Canadian funds,
convert using the current
exchange rate. UNESCO
coupons welcome.)*

☐ **BILL ME LATER:** ($5 service charge will be added)
(Bill-me option is good on US/Canada/Mexico orders only;
not good to jobbers, wholesalers, or subscription agencies.)

☐ Check here if billing address is different from
shipping address and attach purchase order and
billing address information.

Signature_____

☐ **PAYMENT ENCLOSED: $**_____

☐ **PLEASE CHARGE TO MY CREDIT CARD.**

☐ Visa   ☐ MasterCard   ☐ AmEx   ☐ Discover
☐ Diners Club

Account # _____

Exp. Date _____

Signature _____

Prices in US dollars and subject to change without notice.

NAME _____

INSTITUTION _____

ADDRESS _____

CITY _____

STATE/ZIP _____

COUNTRY _____ COUNTY (NY residents only) _____

TEL _____ FAX _____

E-MAIL_____
May we use your e-mail address for confirmations and other types of information? ☐ Yes   ☐ No

Order From Your Local Bookstore or Directly From
The Haworth Press, Inc.
10 Alice Street, Binghamton, New York 13904-1580 • USA
TELEPHONE: 1-800-HAWORTH (1-800-429-6784) / Outside US/Canada: (607) 722-5857
FAX: 1-800-895-0582 / Outside US/Canada: (607) 772-6362
E-mail: getinfo@haworth.com
PLEASE PHOTOCOPY THIS FORM FOR YOUR PERSONAL USE.

BOF96